The NEXT STEP

WHOA, THAT'S GOOD

WISDOM

50 DEVOTIONS TO FIND YOUR WAY FORWARD

Sadie Robertson Huff

WITH DEBBIE WICKWIRE

THOMAS NELSON

Since 1798

Published in Nashville, Tennessee, by Thomas Nelson. Thomas Nelson is a registered trademark of HarperCollins Christian Publishing, Inc.

Thomas Nelson titles may be purchased in bulk for educational, business, fund-raising, or sales promotional use. For information, please email SpecialMarkets@ThomasNelson.com.

Unless otherwise noted, Scripture quotations are taken from the New Century Version®. Copyright © 2005 by Thomas Nelson. Used by permission. All rights reserved.

Scripture quotations marked ESV are taken from the ESV® Bible (The Holy Bible, English Standard Version®). Copyright © 2001 by Crossway, a publishing ministry of Good News Publishers. Used by permission. All rights reserved.

Scripture quotations marked MSG are taken from THE MESSAGE. Copyright © 1993, 2002, 2018 by Eugene H. Peterson. Used by permission of NavPress. All rights reserved. Represented by Tyndale House Publishers, a Division of Tyndale House Ministries.

Scripture quotations marked NIV are taken from the Holy Bible, New International Version®, NIV®. Copyright © 1973, 1978, 1984, 2011 by Biblica, Inc.® Used by permission of Zondervan. All rights reserved worldwide. www.zondervan.com. The "NIV" and "New International Version" are trademarks registered in the United States Patent and Trademark Office by Biblica, Inc.®

Any internet addresses, phone numbers, or company or product information printed in this book are offered as a resource and are not intended in any way to be or to imply an endorsement by Thomas Nelson, nor does Thomas Nelson vouch for the existence, content, or services of these sites, phone numbers, companies, or products beyond the life of this book.

Cover design and art direction by Tiffany Forrester
Photography by Krissy Saleh

ISBN 978-1-4002-2859-1 (HC)
ISBN 978-1-4002-2860-7 (audiobook)
ISBN 978-1-4002-2858-4 (epub)

Printed in Korea

24 25 26 27 28 29 30 PAC 10 9 8 7 6 5 4 3 2 1

CONTENTS

HOW DO WE FIND OUR WAY?

IN MARCH 2021 THE SUEZ CANAL was blocked for six days by the *Ever Given*, one of the largest container ships in the world. Like me, you're probably not an expert in global shipping and logistics. But here's the TL;DR: jamming up the Suez Canal, a waterway that spans 120 miles across the smallest part of Egypt and snakes into the Red Sea, is a *really* huge deal. For container ships traveling from Asia to Europe (or vice versa), going through the Suez Canal instead of around the southern tip of Africa shaves twenty-four days off the journey. That saves companies tons of time and money.

The *Ever Given* is the size of an actual skyscraper, and it can carry 20,000 shipping containers. So obviously, it's a *huge* ship. On March 23 this huge ship was traveling from China to the Netherlands via the Suez Canal when the winds picked up to almost fifty miles per hour and began to dust up sand. The weather was so bad that the captain of the *Ever Given* couldn't see the ship was drifting sideways. When the dust cleared, the captain realized, in shock, that the ship had veered off course and wedged itself perpendicular into the sandy wall of the canal. And the shipping traffic for the entire globe began to back up behind this ship, costing companies around the world almost ten billion dollars a day.[1]

People worked around the clock to clear nearly thirty tons of sand and free the ship; in fact, they had to dig nearly sixty feet deep (that's the length of a regulation bowling lane!) to try to get the ship out. The work wasn't just difficult—it was dangerous. At any moment the ship, which was the size of a ten-story building, could shift its weight and crush the crew working underneath. But all the human toil, engineering knowledge, and modern equipment wasn't enough. The rescue efforts ultimately required a power beyond human control: the tides. High tide raised the water level, which aided the workers, and the ship finally broke free to once again move under its own steam. The Suez rescuers were quickly hailed as heroes, while many villagers thought the rescue was an absolute miracle that defied logic.[2]

———

Have you ever gotten off course? I have. More times than I can count, I've felt *stuck*, like I was unable to change direction from my current path and unsure of where I was supposed to be going even if I *could* change course. (I've also, at times, simply set off in the wrong direction.)

Sometimes we may feel stuck—that's just how life goes. But unlike the *Ever Given*, we're never *not* moving. In fact, we're always moving toward something. That's why it's so important for us to know the way we should be going, so we can keep walking in God's wisdom and doing what He's called us to do. Sometimes this means making big life decisions. But often, it's the little choices we make day after day that create a lifestyle of loving God and walking in His wisdom.

Perhaps you feel like you've lost your way or you're not sure what your next step is. Maybe you're starting your walk with God and need direction on this new journey. Or it's possible you've been walking with Jesus for a long time, but you need a reset. Whichever stuck scenario describes you, I promise that God has a plan and purpose for you. Some of His plans are for all of His children—to become more and more like Christ, to spread the gospel, to make disciples, and to see heaven come to earth. Those big plans are the reason we're here. But our Jesus is also a personal God who loves us deeply and cares about the most intimate details of our lives. He sees your longing for meaningful relationships. He knows your desire for purpose and direction. He recognizes your passions and dreams. And He wants you to know Him and to walk with Him on every step of your journey.

Do you know what I love about the *Ever Given* ship story? It shows us that when people are willing to show up and do the work, God can come in with His divine power and finish the job. It's the same way with us: we need God's power to help us get unstuck, to help us find our way so that we can take the next step forward.

Over the next fifty days together, we will read through verses from the Bible's wisdom books—Job, Psalms, Proverbs, Ecclesiastes, and Song of Songs. I have always been drawn to these books because even though they were written thousands of years ago, they are still applicable to us today. Why? Because after all this time, these books show us how to live a good and righteous life, the way God wants us to live (even the sometimes-hard-to-understand Song of Songs!).

Listen, there's *so* much more to say about these books than what I can fit in these pages. So I'd like to encourage you to grab your own Bible, find the chapter and verse (or verses) for the day, and read them. Spending time in the Word like this will not only help you understand the overall message a bit more, it'll also allow you to savor more of the wisdom from these words. And if you'd like, you can underline or highlight the verses that speak to you. Write notes beside them, along with the date you read them. It will help you make all of this wisdom seem even more personal to you—because it is!

Friend, I'm praying that as you apply God's Word on topics you can relate to your spiritual, mental, and physical life, you'll grow in His grace and knowledge.

At the end of each day is a Find Your Way section to reflect on what you've just read. And at the end of each week is an exercise called Reflect on It, which will give you an opportunity to review the main thought from each of the five previous days. Finally, Rest and Worship—a selection of worship songs intended to help you turn your eyes to the One who leads us in His way—rounds out the week.

I'd like to challenge you to move into a deeper, more active, and more personal relationship with God. Will you join me? Let's do this together as we gain wisdom, live more purposefully, and discover that because Jesus is the Way, we can always move forward with Him.

Grateful to be on this journey with you,

Sadie

1

God's glory is on tour in the skies, God-craft on exhibit across the horizon. Madame Day holds classes every morning, Professor Night lectures each evening.

Their words aren't heard, their voices aren't recorded, but their silence fills the earth; unspoken truth is spoken everywhere.

God makes a huge dome for the sun—a superdome! The morning sun's a new husband leaping from his honeymoon bed, the daybreaking sun an athlete racing to the tape.

That's how God's Word vaults across the skies from sunrise to sunset, melting ice, scorching deserts, warming hearts to faith.

The revelation of GOD is whole and pulls our lives together. The signposts of GOD are clear and point out the right road. The life-maps of GOD are right, showing the way to joy. The directions of GOD are plain and easy on the eyes. GOD's reputation is twenty-four-carat gold, with a lifetime guarantee. The decisions of GOD are accurate down to the nth degree.

God's Word is better than a diamond, better than a diamond set between emeralds. You'll like it better than strawberries in spring, better than red, ripe strawberries.

There's more: God's Word warns us of danger and directs us to hidden treasure. Otherwise how will we find our way? Or know when we play the fool? Clean the slate, God, so we can start the day fresh! Keep me from stupid sins, from thinking I can take over your work; then I can start this day sun-washed, scrubbed clean of the grime of sin. These are the words in my mouth; these are what I chew on and pray. Accept them when I place them on the morning altar, O God, my Altar-Rock, God, Priest-of-My-Altar.

PSALM 19 MSG

Wisdom DAY 1

THE BEST TIME TO SPEND WITH GOD

Clean the slate, God, so we can start the day fresh! Keep me from stupid sins, from thinking I can take over your work; then I can start this day sun-washed, scrubbed clean of the grime of sin. These are the words in my mouth; these are what I chew on and pray. Accept them when I place them on the morning altar, O God, my Altar-Rock, God, Priest-of-My-Altar.

PSALM 19:12–14 MSG

MORNING ROUTINE—THE MOVIE EDITION: You wake up to birds singing. Leisurely stretching, you jump out of bed, grab a comfy blanket and a cup of something hot and delicious, and head to your designated quiet spot where the night before you placed your Bible, your journal, and a pen. You start your day reading, studying, and talking to God in prayer.

Morning routine—the reality show: You wake up and hit the snooze button. After a round or two (or three) of snoozes, you reach for your phone. Bleary-eyed, you scroll through posts and comments, catch up on news stories, and check the weather. You glance at the clock and realize, *Oh my goodness, I'm late!* Then you fall out of bed, knock over the water glass on the nightstand, and step on the dog as you race to the shower, the child, the office, the to-do list.

VERY EARLY IN THE MORNING,
WHILE IT WAS STILL DARK,
JESUS GOT UP, LEFT
THE HOUSE AND WENT
OFF TO A SOLITARY PLACE,
WHERE HE PRAYED.

Mark 1:35 NIV

I don't know about you, but for me, the reality show happens *way* more often than the movie edition.

So how do we start our days with God? And what if spending time with Him were less about the timeframe and more about the relationship?

If the first part of the day is *not* your best part because you're not a morning person, or you work third shift, or you're in a season of life (like I am) where your little ones don't sleep much—or *ever*—then begin with a simple prayer of, *Good morning, Lord!* That's it! Then punctuate moments of your day with quick prayers of, *Thank You,* or, *I love You,* until you get to the quiet-and-alone time that works best for you. Maybe that time is during your drive to work, while you're on the treadmill at the gym, or even when it finally gets quiet in your home at the end of the day.

It's wonderful to start your first fifteen minutes of the day with God. But remember, your relationship with Him is bigger than just those fifteen minutes in the morning. We need more than just quiet times with God—we need a lifestyle that revolves *around* Him to truly have a relationship *with* Him.

I love going on dates with my husband, Christian. While those times when just the two of us get away are certainly important, my relationship with Christian is a 24/7 commitment. It doesn't just happen on a nice dinner date. Our relationship is a lifelong vow represented by the lifestyle we live to honor and love each other well.

> Thank You, heavenly Father, for the gift of grace. Clean my slate, God. Keep me from sin, and help me to spend time with You today and every day. I love You. Amen.

And you know what? I think we can look at our relationship with God the same way.

So what's the best time for you to spend with Him? Any time. All the time. As much time as you can give Him.

True "quiet" time with God is not easy to pull off, but even Jesus needed it and made time for it. The Bible tells us about several times when He went away to pray and spend time with the Father. Those times instructed Jesus, encouraged Him, and refreshed Him.

I love that we don't know all that was said during Jesus' quiet-and-alone times with God. Some moments with the Father are intended to be private. There is such a temptation these days to share everything, but there's something sacred about the time you spend with just your Heavenly Father. And as it benefits and builds you up, it also instills the wisdom you need for when you eventually leave that quiet-and-alone time and interact with others.

Friend, take a deep breath and know that God desires to spend time with you so you can grow in relationship with Him. Let's take time to talk to Him right now.

Find Your WAY

What's the time of day when you're the most still, or when you have the most free time? Think through how you can use that as your quiet-and-alone time with God. If the first part of your day doesn't work, find a block of time that will. Then do your best to stick with it so you can create a routine that will help keep you going. Right now for me, it's my drives to and from work. I protect that time by not calling someone or turning on random music. Instead, I use the time to talk to God and worship Him. Also the mornings I'm up before the kids, or evenings when I stay up after putting them down are great quiet-and-alone moments. These times to worship, read, think, and pray are always so life-giving!

Wisdom DAY 2

CREATIVITY LIVES IN YOU

God's glory is on tour in the skies, God-craft on exhibit across the horizon.

PSALM 19:1 MSG

I ONCE ATTENDED A SONGWRITER'S GATHERING with Chris McClarney, a worship leader best known for his song "Your Love Never Fails."[1] He told us about a day he was trying to write some new music when he prayed, *God, give me the songs of heaven.* He said he felt like God showed up in a very real way and spoke to him, saying something along the lines of, "The songs of heaven are in your heart!"

Chris shared that he felt so much freedom as he realized how true this was. He didn't have to search the heavens to find the songs of God; he simply needed to look in his own heart, where God dwells. That revelation enabled Chris to write the songs that God had already put in him and not be so hard on himself in the creative process.

What a beautiful thought: God has planted creativity in our hearts and in our minds. And He desires to use us to share the songs of heaven with others!

Courtney, who does all the graphics for our ministry, and I have discussed the challenges we face in being innovative and creative. Both of us want to be what God has called us to be, not just a copy of someone else. For Court, this looks like spending time in God's Word, going on walks, and opening her mind

Lord, I don't often feel very creative. But if I believe Your Word that says I am made in Your image, and that before the day of my birth You created me and chose me, then I am simply going to begin praising You for what You have already planted in my heart. Thank You for Your gift of creativity and how it lives out uniquely in each one of us. Amen.

to find the wisdom and insight she needs to make something unique and different—to honor God with the creativity He has placed inside her.

Creativity is what God has put inside all of us. Genesis 1:27 reminds us that we are the image bearers of the ultimate Creator. What an incredible thought that God's creativity is on display in each one of us!

You don't have to be a songwriter or a designer to have creativity inside of you and to enjoy giving it back to God. You may find that painting, poetry, gardening,

drawing, dancing, or some other hobby brings you both joy and relaxation while also being a type of worship. But if you don't think of yourself as creative, I'd love to challenge you to drop the "I'm not" language and just try something. I didn't think I was creative for the longest time because I wasn't an art major like my mom and two sisters were. I may not be the best artist, but I am creative in my own ways. After all, I was created by the Creator of the entire universe who chose me to be me! And if you *are* like my mom and sisters and already love being artistic, consider this your encouragement to embrace that side of yourself even more fully.

Find Your WAY

Answer the questions under the words that apply. Depending on your answer, consider what God has put in you.

I AM CREATIVE.

- What have you created?

- Of those things you've created, what did you most enjoy working on?

- Where do you look for your creative inspiration?

I AM NOT VERY CREATIVE.

- If you could create something, what would it be?

- What content creators on social media offer something you might enjoy or be inspired by?

Wisdom DAY 3

TELL ME THE TRUTH

Madame Day holds classes every morning, Professor Night lectures
each evening. Their words aren't heard, their voices aren't recorded, but
their silence fills the earth: unspoken truth is spoken everywhere.

PSALM 19:2–4 MSG

YOU'RE AT DINNER WITH FRIENDS and notice one of them has something stuck in their teeth. It's super obvious, but you know they'll be embarrassed if you tell them. So what do you do?

The truth is always the most honest and loving response, but sometimes telling the truth can feel awkward, uncomfortable, and even a little offensive. What can be even more challenging is to know what truth even *is*. How do we know what is true in a world that wants to distinguish *my* truth from *your* truth?

Urban Dictionary, which I don't recommend using beyond learning what the culture thinks, defines "my truth" this way:

Non-negotiable personal opinion: Often used by academics, this is a convenient phrase for avoiding arguments because people can contradict your opinion but not your "truth." The phrase is often used when seeking to justify a controversial personal stance or action because people are not allowed to argue with "your truth."[1]

THEN YOU
WILL KNOW
THE TRUTH,
AND THE
TRUTH WILL
MAKE YOU
FREE.

John 8:32

How scary is this? Are we now so entitled to our own opinions that we have no standard for truth? Beyond being scary—and, frankly, ironic—it's also confusing and highlights the urgent need to understand biblical truth.

Here are some questions I ask myself when I'm trying to discern whether or not something is true:

- **Does it line up with the Bible?** Are there multiple verses, passages, or themes that support it as true and in line with God's Word?
- **Have I prayed about it?** Have I asked God directly to show me what is true, and do I have a willing spirit to adjust my behavior—and beliefs—accordingly?
- **Have I sought wise Christian counsel?** People aren't perfect, and they don't have all the answers. You don't need to ask *everyone* for their opinion; instead, direct your questions to a small number of believers who diligently seek the Lord and live in a way that honors Him.

When we allow our feelings to determine what truth is, we can easily make irrational or unwise decisions. We've all had moments when it felt easier to do something comfortable than to do the right thing. The problem is, there are always consequences to our decisions.

Don't live stuck in a place where you're unwilling to see the honest truth about something in your life—a relationship, a habit, a mindset. Until you face the truth, you won't be able to find your way forward to God's wisdom, which brings healing and joy.

> Lord, help me stand strong in Your truth. I know that You and Your Word can be trusted. Thank You for providing Your Spirit to help me know what's true. Amen.

Remember the "friend with stuff in her teeth" scenario I talked about earlier? Well, it actually *happened* to me. The other day I was sitting with friends, and one of them told another that she had food in her teeth. At first my friend felt embarrassed, but she was thankful someone told her. Then she looked at me and said with a little frustration, "Why didn't you tell me?"

I believe we *do* appreciate people who speak the truth to us, even if the truth is hard to hear. You trust the people who are honest with you. So let's not sit here with metaphorical food in our teeth because we don't want to be embarrassed, or we don't want to hear the truth. I'm committed to speaking it, because I'd like the favor returned!

Find Your WAY

The word *truth* can be so confusing because of the "my truth" versus "your truth" lie. What makes truth powerful is that it's *true*—which sounds totally obvious, but it's an important thing we seem to have forgotten. Can you think of ways that truth is being compromised in the world around you? What about in your own personal life? Have you bought into a cultural opinion instead of actual truth?

Consider this: How many of us go to church to get encouraged and feel better about ourselves instead of to be challenged to find a better way of living? We want the self-help book that tells us how to be confident, how to live a productive life, how to feel good—but that's not the message of the gospel, which is transformational. And praise God for that! The gospel is not just a message that puts a Band-Aid on your hurts; it truly heals you and changes you! To be confronted with the Creator exposes you to who you really are. But that is the most beautiful thing, because it's what will lead you to Jesus, who says in John 14:6, "I am the way, and the truth, and the life."

Wisdom DAY 4

LET'S MOVE

God makes a huge dome for the sun—a superdome! The morning sun's a new
husband leaping from his honeymoon bed, the daybreaking sun an athlete
racing to the tape. That's how God's Word vaults across the skies from
sunrise to sunset, melting ice, scorching deserts, warming hearts to faith.

PSALM 19:4–6 MSG

I'M NOT MUCH OF AN EARLY MORNING PERSON, but when I do wake up in time to see a sunrise, the experience reminds me that all of Creation is in constant motion.

Psalm 19 includes a beautiful description of daybreak and of the Creator Himself, who causes the earth to spin on its axis once every twenty-four hours. (At the equator, the earth's rotation clocks in at 1,000 miles per hour![1])

Our bodies were also created to move, which improves our mental health while strengthening us physically. When I entered into an unhealthy season of my life, thanks to issues with a negative body image, I became obsessed with counting calories and working out. Thankfully, the Lord redeemed my view of myself, and I came out of that season. But afterward, I went to the other extreme and didn't care at all about what I ate. I also didn't work out, because exercising reminded me of feeling like I was trapped, chained to all of the reps and the counting. I finally realized that running from the issue wasn't actually the same thing as being free from it. Now, I am truly living in freedom when it comes to food and working out. I didn't find that freedom in a number on the scale, which is constantly fluctuating, or in hitting a certain goal—I found it when God healed my heart. Part of that healing came from confessing to God, my friends, and my family the thoughts and lies I had been struggling with. But it also came from practical things like deleting my calorie-counting app and taking off my Apple Watch for a time.

Thank You, Jesus, for my body and for the ability to be active. Help me to honor this gift by helping me to make wise choices about how I nourish my body and how I move. I trust that You will show me the way. Amen.

And here's the cool part of all this: I've now had two babies, and I am so thankful my heart and mind were set free to embrace my changing body so it could become an amazing host for my daughters.

How about a challenge? If you're not physically active right now, make a plan to start today by walking around your neighborhood. (Don't try to do a marathon the first day or week—just get started and ask God to help you keep going.) Here are a few ideas to help:

- **Decide on a time to move.** My best time to move is in the morning. It puts me in the right frame of mind for the rest of my day. I also love taking a quick walk with the family after work.
- **Set a goal or two.** Not a calorie goal, but a *fun* goal that moving can help you accomplish. For me, while I'm lifting weights, I think of myself lifting up my daughter Haven's car seat as she gets a little heavier. It is fun to think that the weights I am lifting now will help me become stronger as my baby grows.
- **Consider finding a workout partner**. Someone who will keep you honest by showing up every day. This is especially helpful for me!
- **Make it fun!** Change things up so you can have some variety. For instance, there are all kinds of fun dance workouts on YouTube that I love to do.

Find Your WAY

There are lots of fun ways to keep your body moving. Find what works best for you and stick with it. Here are some ideas to get you started:

- I love taking workout classes—spin, boxing, Zumba. Check the gyms in your area and find a class that works for you.

- YouTube workout videos give you an easy way to exercise at home.

- I have friends come over one morning each week. We work out together and then have coffee, and it's become a sweet time of fellowship—plus it's a fun way to get my workout in!

- **Take baby steps.** Realize it takes time to get stronger, but that every step you take is one step closer to feeling better in so many areas of your life.

Always be wise about doing what's best for your body and unique circumstances. For instance, it was nearly three-and-a-half months after I had my older daughter Honey before I started working out again. And it was even longer than that with Haven. So give yourself grace. Again, the goal is being healthy in your mind, body, and spirit!

DON'T YOU KNOW THAT YOU ARE GOD'S TEMPLE AND THAT GOD'S SPIRIT LIVES IN YOU?

1 Corinthians 3:16

Wisdom DAY 5

WHAT YOU THINK BECOMES WHO YOU ARE

The revelation of GOD is whole and pulls our lives together. The signposts of GOD are clear and point out the right road. The life-maps of GOD are right, showing the way to joy.... There's more: God's Word warns us of danger and directs us to hidden treasure.

PSALM 19:7–8, 11 MSG

HAVE YOU EVER BEEN TAKEN BY SURPRISE by an unhealthy, misleading thought? I sure have. You're rolling along through life and then . . .

Whoa! What was that?

A thought pops into your head that's not who you are, what you normally think, and certainly not what you believe. Many people call these "intrusive thoughts." And while we cannot control every thought that pops into our heads, we *can* control how we respond to them. Let's consider how the very first humans handled this.

Adam and Eve were blissfully living in the garden of Eden with no problems, no pain, and no worries. That was, until Satan slithered into their lives to plant an intrusive thought in Eve's mind that the only reason God wouldn't allow the couple to eat the fruit from that one certain tree in the middle of the garden was because He knew that if they did, their eyes would be opened and they would become just like Him. When Satan planted that lie into her mind, Eve didn't shut it down. She

Father, thank You for helping me to stay mindful of what I'm thinking. I choose to not allow my mind to bully me; instead, I want to take captive the thoughts that do not honor You and give them to You. Please fill my mind with Your truth. Amen.

allowed it to take up residence in her head and cause her to act in a way she knew was against God's command. From there, she shared the intrusive thought—*and the fruit*—with Adam, and he also bought into the lie. Then both of their eyes were opened in a way God never intended them to be. Sin entered into their hearts and, consequently, into the hearts of every human to come after them.

Like Eve, we've all struggled with intrusive thoughts planted by the Enemy of our souls. That's why it's essential to recognize these thoughts as soon as possible and address them immediately to prevent them from doing any damage. But how do we do this?

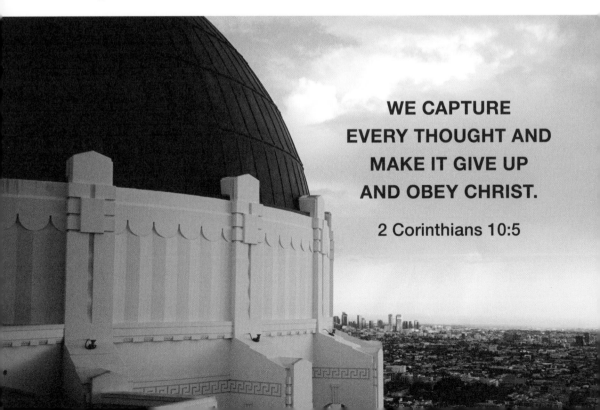

WE CAPTURE EVERY THOUGHT AND MAKE IT GIVE UP AND OBEY CHRIST.

2 Corinthians 10:5

When I need solid direction, I go to the Bible—the ultimate life-map. And if I'm not sure where to go in the Bible, I ask a mentor to guide me to the right scriptures and stories of complicated, messed-up people who I can learn from. Their stories direct me to Jesus and put me on the pathway to joy. I bet the same is true for you!

Plus, along the way are God's signposts that offer direction on our choices and even our thoughts. One of those markers is 2 Corinthians 10:5, which says to "take captive every thought to make it obedient to Christ" (NIV). In other words, if you don't like what your thoughts are saying, you can change the channel, so to speak. Change your focus, and change your thinking. Then start thinking of something you're grateful for.

Don't get bullied by intrusive thoughts. Fight back! Sometimes you need to change your environment by removing yourself from the situation and anything related to it. For sure, you'll need to capture those thoughts by identifying them either verbally or in writing, then pray and ask God to remove them from you.

If you deal with your thoughts aggressively, you can win the battle! I have a friend who often says, "A word is more powerful than a thought." Sometimes when I have intrusive thoughts, I simply have to say out loud that the thought is not true, and then state what I really believe.

Friend, you don't have to stay a victim to your erratic thoughts. That's not who you are. God has already won this battle for us, and He can help us change our thought patterns.

Find Your WAY

Find a quiet spot where you can spend some time reflecting on your daily routines and thought life. Are there any areas of your life where you might be exposing yourself to situations, influences, and thoughts that aren't God-honoring? Consider starting a list in the Notes app on your phone of any area or issue you feel you need to avoid. Remember, writing something down establishes it as a *thing*. An abstract idea solidifies into something real—something you need to be aware of and deal with.

REFLECT on IT

As you reflect on this week, consider what you've learned about finding your way to the life God has mapped out for you. Highlight the statement(s) below that speak to you, then on the journaling lines write notes to yourself so you can remember God's truth and live it out every day.

- Establish dedicated, undistracted time with God so you can connect with Him every day.

- Be who God created you to be, uniquely designed with His creativity living inside of you.

- Seek God's way, His truth, and His Word instead of allowing your own feelings to determine what you believe is true.

- Take ownership of your body so you can physically move toward health and well-being.

- Be aware of any misleading or intrusive thoughts, and take captive any that aren't God-honoring.

_____

_____

_____

REST and WORSHIP

God designed each week to include a day of rest. Use this day to take a time-out from the world and worship Him.

I've found that music is a gift that connects our spirits with God's Holy Spirit, whether we're listening to worship music that turns thoughts toward God, or we hear a song that describes exactly how we're feeling. Here are two of my favorite songs that reflect on what we talked about this week:

- "Presence," by LO Worship

- "Bigger than I Thought," by Passion Music, featuring Sean Curran

Lord, I've loved connecting with You this week. I pray You would continue to open my ears and my mind to hearing what You have to say to me. Amen.

God is our protection and our strength. He always helps in times of trouble. So we will not be afraid even if the earth shakes, or the mountains fall into the sea, even if the oceans roar and foam, or the mountains shake at the raging sea.

Selah.

There is a river that brings joy to the city of God, the holy place where God Most High lives. God is in that city, and so it will not be shaken. God will help her at dawn. Nations tremble and kingdoms shake. God shouts and the earth crumbles.

The Lord All-Powerful is with us; the God of Jacob is our defender.

Selah.

Come and see what the Lord has done, the amazing things he has done on the earth. He stops wars everywhere on the earth. He breaks all bows and spears and burns up the chariots with fire. God says, "Be still and know that I am God. I will be praised in all the nations; I will be praised throughout the earth."

The Lord All-Powerful is with us; the God of Jacob is our defender.

Selah.

PSALM 46

Lord, there is no god like you and no works like yours. Lord, all the nations you have made will come and worship you. They will honor you. You are great and you do miracles. Only you are God. Lord, teach me what you want me to do, and I will live by your truth. Teach me to respect you completely. Lord, my God, I will praise you with all my heart, and I will honor your name forever. You have great love for me. You have saved me from death. . . .

Lord, you are a God who shows mercy and is kind. You don't become angry quickly. You have great love and faithfulness.

PSALM 86:8–13, 15

Wisdom DAY 6

SOLID ROCK FOUNDATION

God is our protection and our strength. He always helps in times of trouble. So we will not be afraid even if the earth shakes, or the mountains fall into the sea, even if the oceans roar and foam, or the mountains shake at the raging sea.

PSALM 46:1–3

MACHU PICCHU IS AN ANCIENT SITE that was unknown to the Western world until 1911, when a Yale University professor named Hiram Bingham discovered it high in the Andes Mountains in Peru. Built around 1450 by the Inca Empire as a palace of sorts for their emperor Pachacuti, the site was abandoned one century later and remained hidden for nearly four hundred years.[1] Today, it's one of the seven wonders of the modern world because of how well it was built and how long it has lasted.[2] In fact, the stones of the buildings were cut so precisely and fit together so well, you can't even insert a credit card between them. But maybe the most remarkable feature of Machu Picchu is that experts estimate that 60 percent of its construction is underground, where the essential site preparation, foundation design, and drainage reside.[3]

The citadel was built with rock on rock, so its foundation and walls are solid. And that's probably how, through centuries of earthquakes and rainy seasons, Machu Picchu has prevailed.

There's a story in Matthew 7 that compares two kinds of people—wise and foolish. The wise man builds his house on rock. The foolish man builds his house on sand. What happened when it rained hard, the floods came, and the wind blew? The house on the sand crashed down, while the house on the rock stood firm.

You see, it matters what kind of foundation we choose to build our lives upon. Consider this: if Machu Picchu didn't have a solid foundation underneath, then almost six hundred years later there would be nothing to see there. So what kind of foundation are you building your life, your family, your home, and your career on? Is it on the sustainability of God and His Word? Or is it on someone else's interpretation of truth, or constantly evolving cultural trends?

> Jesus, You are the solid rock, the foundation I want to build my life and family and work upon. I want to be wise, not foolish, and I want to live for Your glory, not my own. It's hard—I need Your wisdom. Thank You for helping me. Amen.

It's tempting to neglect building a solid foundation for our lives and spend our time working on the things that everybody can see—an impressive platform, awards and trophies, the perfect spouse and kids and life. But going into our prayer closets, spending time reading the Bible, doing our good deeds in secret—those are the things that'll keep us on solid ground when life does its best to shake us.

Christian and I recently built our first house together. One night the builders were preparing to pour the foundation so that it would have time to dry before any rain came the next day. About 2:00 a.m., when we knew they were laying the physical foundation of our home, we got on our knees to pray for our home's spiritual foundation. We've learned that when people come to our house, they're always more impacted by what they *feel* than by what they see. The spiritual foundation is even more perceptible and influential than the concrete beneath their feet.

Find Your WAY

As you build whatever it is you're building in life, remember: don't build it on yourself. Build it on the sustainability of God and His Word. To understand the difference between the two, make a list of your abilities compared to God's abilities. His way is the only way for what you do to outlive you!

I challenge you to let more of what you do be the "unseen things." What you do when no one else is around *will* actually be what determines who you are and if what you're building will be built to last. My constant prayer is that everything I do that others can see is simply an overflow of what God is working inside me.

Oh, and if you ever get to see Machu Picchu in person—and I hope you do—remember, it isn't 50 percent that's underground, it's *60* percent. What is unseen is greater than what is seen.

EVERYONE WHO HEARS MY WORDS AND OBEYS THEM IS LIKE A WISE MAN WHO BUILT HIS HOUSE ON ROCK. IT RAINED HARD, THE FLOODS CAME, AND THE WINDS BLEW AND HIT THAT HOUSE. BUT IT DID NOT FALL, BECAUSE IT WAS BUILT ON ROCK.

Matthew 7:24–25

Wisdom DAY 7

YOU CAN DO THE IMPOSSIBLE

There is a river that brings joy to the city of God, the holy place where God Most High lives. God is in that city, and so it will not be shaken. God will help her at dawn. Nations tremble and kingdoms shake. God shouts and the earth crumbles. The LORD All-Powerful is with us; the God of Jacob is our defender.

PSALM 46:4–7

YESTERDAY WE READ ABOUT MACHU PICCHU and its solid foundation. In 2017 I had the opportunity to go there with my sisters and a few friends. As we walked around, stunned by the incredible beauty of the place, we tried to imagine how the Incas had built it. Like, hold up—think about that for a second. Consider when it was built—almost six hundred years ago, when there was no modern machinery to move the extremely heavy rocks to wherever they needed to go. It seems physically impossible!

Have you ever thought there was no way you could do something because it seemed impossible?

Matthew 17 tells the story of Jesus healing a demon-possessed boy after the disciples were unable to. Afterward, they asked Jesus why they hadn't been able to drive out the evil spirits. Jesus told them it was because they didn't have enough faith. He went on to say, "I tell you the truth, if your faith is as big as a mustard seed, you can say to this mountain, 'Move from here to there,' and it will move. All things will be possible for you" (v. 20).

Wow. Even with faith as small as a tiny mustard seed, all things will be possible.

When God plants dreams in our lives, purposes in our souls, and people in our paths, we can't just assume life is going to be easy and trouble free. There are always forces that come against us. Despite how hard we work and how exhausted we might feel, we still need to maintain faith that God will help us accomplish what He has called us to. I can't imagine how it must have felt for the Incas to start such an enormous and seemingly impossible project without the tools we have today. Yet, they began. Digging the trenches. Planning the drainage. Building the foundation. And stone by stone, they persevered to build a true wonder.

> I know all things are possible, Lord, when we depend on You. Help me to take that leap of faith and trust that You will provide all that's needed for what You call me to do. In Your name I pray, amen.

How much more is possible when we persevere for God? When we take our mustard seeds of faith and, stone by stone, continue with the work in front of us? As Psalm 46 reminds us, the Lord All-Powerful, our Helper and Defender, is with us.

Like one of the roughly 1.5 million people who visit Machu Picchu each year to stand in awe and wonder of the impossible,[1] I want to be part of a body of believers who has so much faith in God that we're constantly working toward wonder. I want to hear people say, "This is crazy! No human could do this—only God could!"

Find Your WAY

What is God doing in your life that seems impossible? Maybe you're thinking, *How can I do this by myself?* Maybe that's not the question you need to be asking. Instead try, *God, what can I do? How can I be faithful to Your calling?* Leave the details up to Him and His perfect timing to provide the wisdom, direction, and resources you'll need. Then, when people see what has been accomplished, they'll know it was only because of God—because no human could ever do that. That accomplishment will be its own brand of amazing that fits you and God perfectly!

Wisdom DAY 8

SUPER PLANNER OR CONTROL FREAK?

Come and see what the LORD has done, the amazing things he has done on the earth. He stops wars everywhere on the earth. He breaks all bows and spears and burns up the chariots with fire. God says, "Be still and know that I am God. I will be praised in all the nations; I will be praised throughout the earth." The LORD All-Powerful is with us; the God of Jacob is our defender.

PSALM 46:8–11

I TEND TO PANIC WHEN I'M NOT PREPARED, but who knew that my overpreparedness would lead me to becoming even more fearful?

I preach and speak at a lot of different events. It doesn't matter if I'm speaking to sixty people or sixty thousand—I am going to make sure I'm totally prepared. But I've found that when I try to preach my prepared notes *perfectly*, there is not as much power in the message as when I simply speak from the overflow of my heart. Yes, preparation is a beautiful thing, but only if it's not tied to perfectionism. If I'm truly prepared, then all of my preparation frees me.

There is beauty in preparation, but we *have to* rest in the fact that God is in control, and we're not. Think about when you're flying in an airplane—the way you look at the landscape changes (literally, since you're looking at it from above) and you can see the earth's overall connectedness. Heaven's perspective is the same way. The Bible says right now we see a dim reflection as though we're looking in a mirror, but someday we'll see clearly (1 Corinthians 13:12). Only God can see the whole picture of our lives—and all of eternity.

During the process of writing this book, I was approaching the birth of our second child, Haven Belle. Many of you have heard me tell the story of how overprepared I was for my labor with Honey. I made the "perfect" birth plan after hours of reading, talking to other moms, and practicing my breathing. I decided I didn't want to get induced or have an epidural. Let me just tell you, nothing about Honey's birth went as planned. She ended up getting stuck, and I *needed* that induction and epidural to complete the birthing process. Looking back I am so glad my plans didn't work out, and God's did.

I went into Haven's birth with this new mindset: the God who formed me and knew me and my two daughters, the One who parted the Red Sea for the Israelites to cross, has shown me that He is always with me and I can put my faith and trust in Him. I had a C-section for her birth, and you know what? God was just as present with me in the room at Haven's birth as He was with me at Honey's.

Father, I trust You. In faith I want to partner with You. Whether in big things, like life decisions, or in little things, like what we should do for dinner, I look to You, knowing You are God. You know what I do not. Help me as I live and work and wait on You. Thank You, Father. Amen.

AS THE HEAVENS ARE
HIGHER THAN THE
EARTH, SO ARE MY
WAYS HIGHER THAN
YOUR WAYS AND MY
THOUGHTS THAN
YOUR THOUGHTS.

Isaiah 55:9 NIV

While it's okay to make plans of your own, try not to hold them so tightly. Instead, be still and realize God is the ultimate defender. Be willing to surrender your own plans, and put your faith and trust in Him. Cast your cares on Him, knowing that He cares about every single detail of your life. It's the only way fear vanishes and real peace lives.

Find Your WAY

Do you tend to be an overplanner? Take some time to think through a few different scenarios where things didn't go as planned. How did you respond? Then, take a moment to think of anything in your life you might be holding too tightly. Raise your hands with open palms, and hand those things over to God.

Wisdom DAY 9

RULES VS. RELATIONSHIP

*Lord, there is no god like you and no works like yours. Lord, all the nations you have made will come and worship you. They will honor you. You are great and you do miracles. Only you are God. L*ORD*, teach me what you want me to do, and I will live by your truth. Teach me to respect you completely. . . . Lord, you are a God who shows mercy and is kind. You don't become angry quickly. You have great love and faithfulness.*

PSALM 86:8–11, 15

C. S. LEWIS WAS ONE OF THE INTELLECTUAL GIANTS of the twentieth century, as well as one of the world's most influential writers. An Oxford professor, Lewis wrote more than thirty books, including *Mere Christianity, The Screwtape Letters,* and *The Chronicles of Narnia*, that have reached a widespread audience and helped many to find their faith in Jesus.[1]

Lewis became a Christian in 1931, at age thirty-three. And I was shocked to learn that, even with his long list of accomplishments in the faith, he didn't discover the principle of God's grace until twenty years after he put his trust in the Lord—which was after he'd written most of his beloved books.

So what *is* grace, anyway?

The basic answer is grace is *the undeserved favor of God*, the forgiveness we receive when we accept that Jesus died on the cross to save us from our sins. But the story doesn't end with our conversion, and it's not just head knowledge. Because while wisdom can grow your *knowledge* of God, it is your understanding of grace that will grow your *relationship* with God.

As a fifty-three-year-old, Lewis discovered the depth of this relationship that provides not only the words of forgiveness but the power to live it out. When he decided he wasn't going to lead a rules-oriented life of trying to be good enough, he began to have a joyful relationship with the God of the universe![2]

Remember how I said I tend to struggle with perfectionism? That's why I *really* need grace. Grace is an essential part of my relationship with God, because without it I would constantly feel the shame of not being enough. With it I know I am radically loved, just as I am.

Thank You, Jesus, for Your ultimate sacrifice of dying on the cross to cover my sins, and for the grace that it offers. Thank You also for the power of grace to live daily—that it's not about keeping the rules, it's about being in relationship with You. Amen.

So many people see the Bible as a rule book with a long list of dos and don'ts. Instead, the Bible speaks of a relationship between a loving God and His creation. There are so many stories in both the Old and New Testaments of people who struggled, failed, and then tried again. They show us that there's no such thing as perfection in us humans—only progress.

In James K. A. Smith's book *You Are What You Love*, Smith explained that the way to get people to build a boat is not to tell them to go get wood, but to teach them to desire the sea.[3] In the same way, if you look at your relationship with God as something you *have to* do, like following a rule (or, you know, having to get up early and chop wood for a boat), then you'll struggle. Instead, when you possess a desire to experience something, like the beauty of the ocean or a relationship with the God of the universe, nothing will stop you from the joy of waking up, going to get the wood, and building that boat.

Every believer's story is of grace that provides forgiveness, transformation, and an ongoing relationship with the Creator of the universe. And when you, like C. S. Lewis, are able to fully grasp and understand grace and God's unending love, you'll find every *I need to* turns into an *I want to*—and every *I have to* into an *I get to.*

Find Your WAY

Is your view of God more about the rules, or is it more about your relationship with Him? Remember that grace isn't a "check-the-box" thing with a license to do whatever you want. Instead, the switch from rules to relationship should help you have a deeper desire to love God and walk in His ways even more.

Wisdom DAY 10

DADDY'S GOT YOU

Lord, my God, I will praise you with all my heart, and I will honor your name forever. You have great love for me. You have saved me from death.

PSALM 86:12–13

CHRISTIAN AND I WERE IN A GOLF CART, driving across my parents' property, with Honey wrapped in his arms. Christian asked her, "Who's got you?" She sweetly replied, "Daddy's got me!" I nearly melted, and for sure I was grateful. Not just for my husband, but for the reminder that God, our Father in heaven, also has us in His firm grip and embrace.

We were made for relationship. And since the world can be such a hard place, we need the comfort of a loving Father who sees us, understands us, and cares about what happens to us. That's where "Daddy's got me" comes in.

Maybe you didn't grow up having an earthly father's love. If so, please allow me to wrap you in a sister-to-sister hug that says, "I'm so sorry." Then I want you to remember our Psalm for today, which reminds us that the God of the universe, our heavenly Father, has great love for you!

When I need a reminder that my heavenly Father's got me, these are some of my go-to verses:

God, my heavenly Father, I thank You for Your constant love and grace, whether I've always felt it or not. In the future, help me to be more aware that You truly have me in Your arms. Help me to feel Your embrace. Amen.

- "So don't worry, because I am with you. Don't be afraid, because I am your God. I will make you strong and will help you; I will support you with my right hand that saves you" (Isaiah 41:10).
- "Remember that I commanded you to be strong and brave. Don't be afraid, because the LORD your God will be with you everywhere you go" (Joshua 1:9).
- "Teach them to obey everything that I have taught you, and I will be with you always, even until the end of this age" (Matthew 28:20).

- "'The virgin will be pregnant. She will have a son, and they will name him Immanuel,' which means God is with us" (Matthew 1:22–23).

On the golf cart that day, it was amazing to see the confidence and the peace Honey rested in after saying, "Daddy's got me." If you ever start feeling alone, forgotten, defeated, or filled with doubt, then remember Daddy, your Heavenly Father, has definitely got you!

Find Your WAY

Whether or not you've felt the love of an earthly father, you can know the love of your heavenly Father. Think back on key moments of your life, and write down some times God wrapped His arms around you and held you, helped you, and let you feel His love through a difficult or scary experience. Then thank Him for it!

REFLECT on IT

As you reflect on the week, consider what you've learned about finding your way to the life God has mapped out for you. Highlight the statement(s) below that speak to you, then on the journaling lines write notes to yourself so you can remember God's truth and live it out every day.

- Build whatever you are building on Jesus, the solid Rock, making sure that what is unseen is greater than what is seen.

- The impossible is made possible when God calls you to it.

- Surrender your own plans, and partner with God as you put your faith and trust in Him.

- The Bible isn't intended to be a rule book with a long list of dos and don'ts, but a love story between God and His creation.

- You never have to feel alone when you remember that God, your Heavenly Father, has got you!

_____

_____

_____

REST and WORSHIP

God designed each week to include a day of rest. Use this day to take a time-out from the world and worship Him.

I've found that music is a gift that connects our spirits with God's Holy Spirit, whether we're listening to worship music that turns thoughts toward God, or we hear a song that describes exactly how we're feeling. Here are two of my favorite songs that reflect on what we talked about this week:

- "Canvas and Clay," by Pat Barrett, featuring Ben Smith

- "All My Hope," by Crowder, featuring Tauren Wells

Lord, I choose to surrender to Your will and Your way. Thank You for being my Father, my Rock, my Redeemer, my strength, and the source of my joy. With You I know nothing is impossible. Lead me in paths of right living, and protect me from the Evil One as I live to serve You all the days of my life. Amen.

3

My child, do not forget my teaching, but keep my commands in mind. Then you will live a long time, and your life will be successful.

Don't ever forget kindness and truth. Wear them like a necklace. Write them on your heart as if on a tablet. Then you will be respected and will please both God and people.

Trust the LORD with all your heart, and don't depend on your own understanding. Remember the LORD in all you do, and he will give you success.

Don't depend on your own wisdom. Respect the LORD and refuse to do wrong. Then your body will be healthy, and your bones will be strong.

Honor the LORD with your wealth and the firstfruits from all your crops. Then your barns will be full, and your wine barrels will overflow with new wine.

My child, do not reject the LORD's discipline, and don't get angry when he corrects you. The LORD corrects those he loves, just as parents correct the child they delight in.

Happy is the person who finds wisdom, the one who gets understanding. Wisdom is worth more than silver; it brings more profit than gold. Wisdom is more precious than rubies; nothing you could want is equal to it. With her right hand wisdom offers you a long life, and with her left hand she gives you riches and honor. Wisdom will make your life pleasant and will bring you peace. As a tree produces fruit, wisdom gives life to those who use it, and everyone who uses it will be happy.

The LORD made the earth, using his wisdom. He set the sky in place, using his understanding. With his knowledge, he made springs flow into rivers and the clouds drop rain on the earth.

My child, hold on to wisdom and good sense. Don't let them out of your sight. They will give you life and beauty like a necklace around your neck. Then you will go your way in safety, and you will not get hurt. When you lie down, you won't be afraid; when you lie down, you will sleep in peace. You won't be afraid of sudden trouble; you won't fear the ruin that comes to the wicked, because the Lord will keep you safe. He will keep you from being trapped.

Whenever you are able, do good to people who need help. If you have what your neighbor asks for, don't say, "Come back later. I will give it to you tomorrow." Don't make plans to hurt your neighbor who lives nearby and trusts you. Don't accuse a person for no good reason; don't accuse someone who has not harmed you.

Don't be jealous of those who use violence, and don't choose to be like them. The Lord hates those who do wrong, but he is a friend to those who are honest. The Lord will curse the evil person's house, but he will bless the home of those who do right. The Lord laughs at those who laugh at him, but he gives grace to those who are not proud. Wise people will receive honor, but fools will be disgraced.

PROVERBS 3

Wisdom DAY 11

THE 24-HOUR RULE

My child, do not forget my teaching, but keep my commands in mind. Then
you will live a long time, and your life will be successful. Don't ever forget
kindness and truth. Wear them like a necklace. Write them on your heart as if
on a tablet. Then you will be respected and will please both God and people.

PROVERBS 3:1–4

FOR A TIME, I LIVED WITH TWO OF MY BEST FRIENDS. Right up front we all three agreed to abide by what we called "24-Hour Rule." If you had a problem with one of the other roommates, you had to address it within twenty-four hours. If you chose not to, then you had to let go of the problem. The rule was honesty, truth, and kindness in action.

You can see the importance of having a practice like this in a shared living space. But any time you're in close proximity with other people, you'll eventually face conflict. It's why the 24-Hour Rule is important in every group dynamic—roommates, family, work, church, and friends.

For instance, think about working in an office. If a team can't decide how to split the responsibilities on a new project and they don't communicate with each other, then they aren't able to be an effective team. In other scenarios maybe someone says something hurtful to you. Maybe someone betrays your trust. Someone borrows money and forgets to repay you. Whatever the issue,

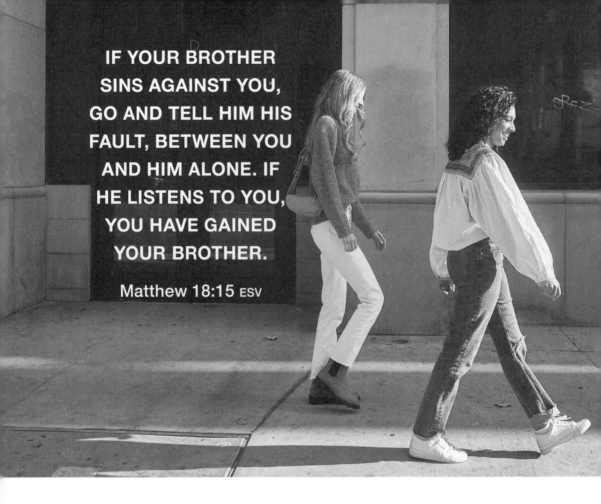

IF YOUR BROTHER
SINS AGAINST YOU,
GO AND TELL HIM HIS
FAULT, BETWEEN YOU
AND HIM ALONE. IF
HE LISTENS TO YOU,
YOU HAVE GAINED
YOUR BROTHER.

Matthew 18:15 ESV

you can be sure that scripture offers guidance on how to move forward. Here are a few examples:

- "A gentle answer will calm a person's anger, but an unkind answer will cause more anger" (Proverbs 15:1).
- "Do to others what you would want them to do to you" (Luke 6:31).
- "When you talk, do not say harmful things, but say what people need—words that will help others become stronger. Then what you say will do good to those who listen to you" (Ephesians 4:29).
- "Be kind and loving to each other, and forgive each other just as God forgave you in Christ" (Ephesians 4:32).
- "When you do things, do not let selfishness or pride be your guide. Instead, be humble and give more honor to others than to yourselves" (Philippians 2:3).

- "Do not be interested only in your own life, but be interested in the lives of others" (Philippians 2:4).

The 24-Hour Rule is also an obvious must for marriage. You've heard the saying, "Don't ever go to bed angry." Did you know it's biblical? Ephesians 4:26 tells us, "When you are angry, do not sin, and be sure to stop being angry before the end of the day." That sounds like "before bed" to me!

The 24-Hour Rule is the road to freedom and another way to get unstuck. If your disagreement is a super big deal, give it forty-eight hours, but make sure you deal with it. And do it in the spirit of God's wisdom and instruction. Working through the issue will be totally worth it.

Find Your WAY

Think of a time when a conflict between you and someone else was resolved quickly because you dealt with it right away, both wisely and kindly. Addressing the issue may not have been easy at the time, but now it's over. Use this experience to develop an intentional plan for any "next time" occurrences. Then, think of a scenario where you did not address a situation and it's still out there, dangling in the wind, threatening to ruin your day. What can you do *now* to resolve this situation? Read the verses above to give you the perspective you need, then ask God to help you.

Dear God, handling conflict is hard, but I know it's important. I need Your help to recognize when I need to say something and also how to do so with kindness and truth. And if I just need to let it go, give me the strength to take a deep breath and move on. Thank You. Amen.

Wisdom DAY 12

ARE YOU LISTENING?

Trust the LORD with all your heart, and don't depend on your own understanding. Remember the LORD in all you do, and he will give you success. Don't depend on your own wisdom. Respect the LORD and refuse to do wrong. Then your body will be healthy, and your bones will be strong.

PROVERBS 3:5–8

"LORD, IF MY NEXT BABY IS A GIRL, what am I going to name her?"

I wasn't even pregnant when I asked that question. But because Christian and I felt God had given us the perfect, meaningful name for Honey, naming my next baby had been on my mind for "if" we had another child.

That day Christian and I were on a flight together, and I was deep in thought. Looking out at the clouds, a name totally dropped into my mind and my heart. *Haven Belle.* I loved it! But I was also surprised, because those names hadn't been on the baby name list I'd been keeping since high school. *Haven* means "safe place or refuge," and *Belle* means "beautiful." The name was much like Honey's—perfect and so very meaningful. Four months later, we found out we were expecting baby number two. Then the gender reveal party brought everything full circle—we were having another girl!

A few months later I noticed a trend on Instagram, where people would post a picture of the first date they had with their spouse. On our first date, Christian

> **Father, I love You and trust You, and I don't want to live a day without You! Thank You for having a plan for me and for caring about every detail of my life. Fine-tune the ears of my spirit so that I can clearly hear Your voice. I am listening. Amen.**

and I had walked by a pottery place and randomly decided to go in. We each decorated a coffee mug. I painted my mug blue and wrote the word *honey* on it because of a verse we'd read together in Proverbs 16:24, which describes pleasant words as being like a honeycomb. *Honey* wasn't on my baby name list, either—it simply described Christian's words to me that were so sweet and healing as he helped me move on from some things in my past. As a shock to us both, there on a coffee mug, in the middle of a photo of our first date, was our first daughter's name: Honey. The only other photo taken during that first date was of the two of us standing under a banner flag with the word *Haven* on it. I. Kid. You. Not!

It's mind-boggling to think that on our first date, God knew Honey and Haven would be born, though the reality is that He was already writing *their* stories long before that. I could have named my daughters anything, and it would have been special. But because I asked and listened for the Father's response, I was able to partner with Him in naming them. (And be blown away all those years later by something that truly strengthened my faith!)

Dear friend, from before the beginning of the earth, God has had you and me in mind. He has been thinking about us and designing us with intention, purpose, and a plan. As we learn to listen to His still, small voice, we begin to recognize that we are loved and cared for more than we can imagine! It's why we can trust Him with our whole hearts. It's why we can lean on His understanding instead of our own. He came before us, He understands the present more completely than we can fathom, and He holds the future. Whatever you're facing today, hand over your understanding of the situation to God—who sees all things—and listen as you lean fully on His wisdom.

God really does have a plan for your life, a plan for good. He is such a good Father!

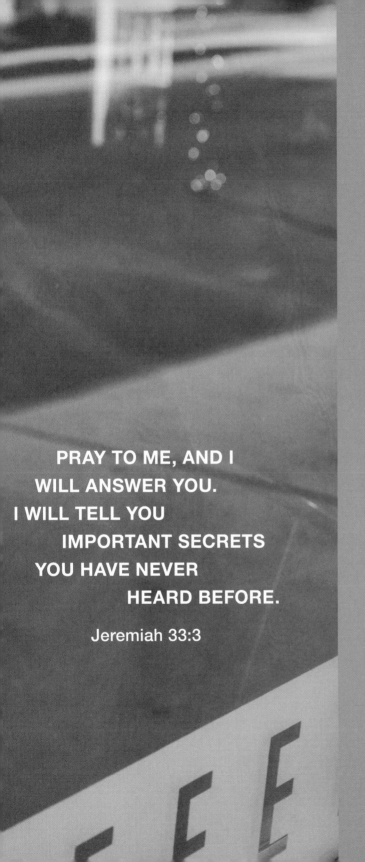

**PRAY TO ME, AND I
WILL ANSWER YOU.
I WILL TELL YOU
IMPORTANT SECRETS
YOU HAVE NEVER
HEARD BEFORE.**

Jeremiah 33:3

Find Your WAY

Can you remember a time when you felt like you heard from the Lord? Maybe not an audible voice , but a knowing inside of you that what you were thinking came directly from Him? If not, pray and ask God that in His time, He would reveal Himself to you in a way that you would know beyond all knowing that it *is* from Him. Ask Him questions and listen for a response. Note the peace that you feel. And look for the evidence.

Wisdom DAY 13

WHAT'S MOST IMPORTANT?

Happy is the person who finds wisdom, the one who gets understanding. Wisdom is worth more than silver; it brings more profit than gold. Wisdom is more precious than rubies; nothing you could want is equal to it. With her right hand wisdom offers you a long life, and with her left hand she gives you riches and honor. Wisdom will make your life pleasant and will bring you peace. As a tree produces fruit, wisdom gives life to those who use it, and everyone who uses it will be happy.

PROVERBS 3:13–18

WE'VE ALL HAD TO FACE DIFFICULT DECISIONS. You're out with friends, and someone has an idea to do something that is over the line you've drawn for yourself. Do you go to the party? Do you say yes to the movie choice? Do you share in the food and drink and whatever else is available? Are you going out with the group or are you staying home? Are you in or are you out? Is it a yes or a no?

Some choices are always going to be harder than others. This is why wisdom is so essential. In fact, our verses today tell us that wisdom is worth more than silver, gold, rubies, or anything else you can think of. Verse 17 even goes so far as to say, "Wisdom will make your life pleasant and will bring you peace."

One of my first opportunities to need that kind of wisdom on my own was as a young teen representing USA Basketball in Austria. I didn't join my teammates for parties and nights out, and I was made fun of. *A lot*. It was lonely. But at the closing Olympic-like ceremony, when I was asked to stand in front of athletes from all of those nations and present an award to the USA Basketball coach, I realized my choices had made a huge difference. God showed me the power of my faith and how it can influence those around me. Even my coach told me, "There's something different about you."

Thank You, Jesus, for the promises in Your Word and for the wisdom that comes with knowing You. I pray You would help me with my life choices. Always keep me mindful of You. Amen.

I didn't know it then, but my thirteen-year-old self was teaching future me a lesson I would hold on to for years: standing with Jesus always pays off. In my first book, *Live Original*, I wrote, "Five seconds of awkward can save you from a lifetime of regret."[1] I must admit, I felt a little awkward sitting by the door during

Find Your WAY

We often look at things through the lens of big life decisions or right-and-wrong scenarios. But walking in wisdom can also look like the small, daily choices we make, such as:

- Putting down our phones and paying attention to the people around us.

- Turning off the TV and having a conversation with our spouse, child, or friend.

- Going for a walk when we don't feel like it, or choosing to turn on the music and literally dance through our bad day.

- Taking a nap when we really need it.

These are a few things on my list. What's on yours?

team parties. My choice didn't feel fun or heroic. It felt a little lame and lonely, but looking back I have absolutely no regrets. I am proud of who I was becoming. In many ways, that time helped shape who I was able to be when I was on *Dancing with the Stars* a few years later, a time when I also had to make decisions that felt a little lame for the sake of staying true to my values.

It's funny how I thought leaving my teenage years behind and becoming an adult would make choices like this easier, but that's not always the case. Now, in a very different way, there are decisions I have to make as a mom and an adult that challenge me with those same feelings. Am I going to watch the shows everyone else is watching so I can stay relevant, even if they're against my morals? Am I going to abide by the cool Gen Z mom way of doing things, or am I going to raise my kids with the values I know are best for their lives—even if they may seem a little old-fashioned? I have to parent with confidence even though the crowd may be doing something different.

I pray that whatever comes your way, you find the wisdom and strength to choose what's most important.

Wisdom DAY 14

BE WISE, STAY SAFE

The LORD made the earth, using his wisdom. He set the sky in place, using his understanding. With his knowledge, he made springs flow into rivers and the clouds drop rain on the earth. My child, hold on to wisdom and good sense. Don't let them out of your sight. They will give you life and beauty like a necklace around your neck. Then you will go your way in safety, and you will not get hurt. When you lie down, you won't be afraid; when you lie down, you will sleep in peace. You won't be afraid of sudden trouble; you won't fear the ruin that comes to the wicked, because the LORD will keep you safe. He will keep you from being trapped.

PROVERBS 3:19–26

HAVE YOU EVER FOUND YOURSELF IN A SITUATION where you didn't feel safe? Unfortunately, I have—multiple times. And what I've learned is that the little decisions we make along the way can make a big difference.

I was in a mall once in Nashville when I noticed three men were following me. I didn't feel good about it, but when I didn't see them for a while, I figured it had either been my imagination or they had left. Later, though, I started feeling nervous about walking alone to my car in the parking garage. My gut said something was off, so I called my dad. He's not much of a phone guy, so I was grateful he answered. I told him where I was and that I was feeling weird and wanted to stay on the phone with him until I was safe. Sure enough, as I was

WHEN I AM AFRAID,
I WILL TRUST YOU.
I PRAISE GOD FOR HIS WORD.
I TRUST GOD,
SO I AM NOT AFRAID.
WHAT CAN HUMAN BEINGS
DO TO ME?

Psalm 56:3–4

talking to him, around the corner I saw a white van and, standing beside it, were the men who had been following me in the mall. The only other vehicle on that level was my car. And the white van was parked right beside it.

What happened next could only be the hand of God. I made eye contact with the men, who became startled and jumped back! I knew God was with me in that moment, and I will always wonder what they saw that made them jump. I immediately turned around and went back inside the mall to find a security guard. I told her about the men who had been following me and were now waiting in a van by my car. She went with me back to the parking garage, but the van was gone.

The guard told me that so many women think they can just go fast and make it to their vehicle, but often they can't. As these women turn to open the door to their vehicle, assailants jump on them. So if you find yourself in the same boat someday (I really hope you don't), I have some advice: call a friend, or find a security guard or a store employee and ask them to walk with you to your vehicle.

I'm not telling you this story to scare you; I just want you to be aware of what could happen—and so often *does* happen to unsuspecting girls and women. I know that God kept me safe that night, but since that night I've learned some practical things that could've also helped me in that situation:

> Thank You, Father, for all You have given me—food, clothing, shelter, and angels to watch over me! Because of Your covering, I will not fear. I know that You not only go with me, You go before me and will come after me. I put my life in Your hands. Amen.

- **Be aware of your surroundings.** For instance, now I don't look at my phone when I'm walking in public alone, especially in a parking lot. I make eye contact with people and stay aware of where I am. If I'm talking on the phone, I tell that person exactly where I am and where I intend to go.

Find Your WAY

My friend Demi Tebow found herself in a frightening situation in June 2017 when she was carjacked in South Africa after being crowned Miss Universe. Though she was eventually able to run away, the five armed attackers now had her keys, which included the key to her house. Demi survived the assault thanks to the self defense class she took from Women Empowered along with the other contestants. Consider taking some classes and becoming knowledgeable on how to protect yourself so that you can walk with more confidence.

- **Don't get too comfortable.** Keep up your guard, even if you're in a familiar area.
- **Trust your instincts.** If something doesn't feel right, then stop, observe the situation, and be smart.
- **Stick together.** If possible, especially at night, ask a friend to join you. Stay in groups and in well-lit places.
- **Be prepared**. Always have something with you to protect yourself—pepper spray, a loud horn, or even a bright light can make a difference.
- **Be equipped**. Take a self-defense class so you'll know how to protect yourself in a physical attack.

So many of us have stories like this. Again, always be alert and listen to that inner voice when it tells you something is wrong. I don't want you to live in a state of fear, but traumatic incidents are a reality all over the world.

Today's verses remind us that God is in charge of all things, including our safety. We can rest in Him and "hold on to wisdom and good sense" (Proverbs 3:21), with an emphasis on caution and prevention—not paranoia—and exercising discernment in how we live. Using wisdom can bring you so much confidence and help you fight against fear!

Wisdom DAY 15

GENEROSITY IS CALLING

Whenever you are able, do good to people who need help. If you have what your neighbor asks for, don't say, "Come back later. I will give it to you tomorrow."

PROVERBS 3:27–28

JIMMY DARTS IS A SELF-DESCRIBED "CRAZY PERSON." Well-known for his random acts of generosity with strangers, Jimmy is a guy who loves Jesus and people, a combo that's filled him with an animated and contagious joy.

His spirit of giving began with his parents. At Christmas, Jimmy's parents would give each of their kids $200—$100 to keep and $100 to give away. With this practice, giving became second nature to the kids and strangers didn't seem so scary.

Jimmy filmed his first kindness video in Miami, where he met a homeless man living on the beach.

"Hey bro," Jimmy said, "do you wanna be best friends for the day?"

The man said, "Yeah, I got nothing else to do."

They played basketball, rollerbladed around, got some food, and just hung out. On the way back the man broke down in tears, saying he'd honestly been struggling with suicidal thoughts that day and had wanted to end his life, but Jimmy had helped change his whole perspective. Jimmy had filmed the highlights of the day, and, before posting the video online, asked the man if by chance he had a cash app. He did, so at the end of the video Jimmy posted a note encouraging viewers to donate to the man. When Jimmy went to bed that night, the video had around 10,000 views. By the next morning, it had more than 15 million views, and the man had received more than $30,000!

Jimmy says the best advice he ever received was from a friend who told him, "Jimmy, you got to be Santa Claus in private before you can be Santa Claus in public."[1] Jimmy spent years giving privately before he ever posted any public giving. And even though he now has millions of followers, he doesn't create

videos to go viral—he creates them to promote generosity. Jimmy knows the names and life stories of the people he's given to, and he still is in contact with many of them.

Though Jimmy's generosity journey may have begun with random acts of giving away money, the road doesn't end there. Jimmy says, "To do this, I have to kick it with Jesus to make sure my heart is right, to be led to the right people, and to partner with Him. I'm not just making a video; I'm talking to a human, a soul that has eternal value, and I am seeing if heaven can invade their life story and restore them."[2]

Generosity is not just a calling for Jimmy Darts—it's a calling for all of us. And it's not just money you can be generous with. You can give your time, help others, bring someone a meal, ask a person how you can pray for them, even simply smile at those you pass by. Let's go spread some kindness today, let our little lights shine, and have a good time doing it.

Find Your WAY

Most everything we see around us in our culture is selfish and self-centered, which is why generosity and kindness are so powerful. But remember that generosity doesn't only have to be about giving money away. Like Jimmy challenged us, the next time you're standing in the grocery store checkout line, tell the person behind you, "Hey, please go in front of me." It'll likely shake them, and they'll be so confused—in an amazing way. Start being generous in any way you can, and you'll be amazed how God opens the door for more acts of generosity.

REFLECT on IT

As you reflect on the week, consider what you've learned about finding your way to the life God has mapped out for you. Highlight the statement(s) below that speak to you, then on the journaling lines write notes to yourself so you can remember God's truth and live it out every day.

- When it comes to personal conflict, commit to living by the 24-Hour Rule.

- Don't depend on your own understanding of things. Ask God to show you His view, then listen and trust Him with all your heart.

- In every situation, rely on God's wisdom to choose what's most important.

- Always be alert and aware of your surroundings—use common sense as you allow the Scriptures to guide you and help you trust God in every circumstance.

- Ask God for a wise and generous heart, looking for ways to do good for people who need help.

_____

_____

_____

REST and WORSHIP

God designed each week to include a day of rest. Use this day to take a time-out from the world and worship Him.

Worship is such a beautiful thing, because we raise our souls to God—and this practice also benefits us. We gain strength, perspective, hope, and love as we worship Him. Here are two of my favorite worship songs for this week:

- "More than Able," by Elevation Worship, featuring Chandler Moore and Tiffany Hudson

- "Look Around," by Housefires, featuring Cecily Hennigan

Thank You, Father, for teaching me to look to You for everything I need. Also, thank You for Your daily provision and protection as I learn to trust You more. Give me Your wisdom to make the right choices. And speak to me in the coming days as together we work through the sometimes-challenging story of Job. I love You. Amen.

Then the LORD answered Job from the storm. He said: . . . "Who shut the doors to keep the sea in when it broke through and was born, when I made the clouds like a coat for the sea and wrapped it in dark clouds, when I put limits on the sea and put its doors and bars in place, when I said to the sea, 'You may come this far, but no farther; this is where your proud waves must stop'?

JOB 38:1, 8–11

Then Job answered the LORD:

"I know that you can do all things and that no plan of yours can be ruined. You asked, 'Who is this that made my purpose unclear by saying things that are not true?' Surely I spoke of things I did not understand; I talked of things too wonderful for me to know. You said, 'Listen now, and I will speak. I will ask you questions, and you must answer me.' My ears had heard of you before, but now my eyes have seen you. So now I hate myself; I will change my heart and life. I will sit in the dust and ashes."

After the LORD had said these things to Job, he said to Eliphaz the Temanite, "I am angry with you and your two friends, because you have not said what is right about me, as my servant Job did. Now take seven bulls and seven male sheep, and go to my servant Job, and offer a burnt offering for yourselves. My servant Job will pray for you, and I will listen to his prayer. Then I will not punish you for being foolish. You have not said what is right about me, as my servant Job did." So Eliphaz the Temanite, Bildad the Shuhite, and Zophar the Naamathite did as the LORD said, and the LORD listened to Job's prayer.

After Job had prayed for his friends, the LORD gave him success again. The

LORD gave Job twice as much as he had owned before. Job's brothers and sisters came to his house, along with everyone who had known him before, and they all ate with him there. They comforted him and made him feel better about the trouble the LORD had brought on him, and each one gave Job a piece of silver and a gold ring.

The LORD blessed the last part of Job's life even more than the first part. Job had fourteen thousand sheep, six thousand camels, a thousand teams of oxen, and a thousand female donkeys. Job also had seven sons and three daughters. He named the first daughter Jemimah, the second daughter Keziah, and the third daughter Keren-Happuch. There were no other women in all the land as beautiful as Job's daughters. And their father Job gave them land to own along with their brothers.

After this, Job lived one hundred forty years. He lived to see his children, grandchildren, great-grandchildren, and great-great-grandchildren. Then Job died; he was old and had lived many years.

JOB 42

Wisdom DAY 16

WHERE WERE YOU?

Then the LORD answered Job from the storm. . . . "Who shut the doors to keep
the sea in when it broke through and was born, when I made the clouds like
a coat for the sea and wrapped it in dark clouds, when I put limits on the sea
and put its doors and bars in place, when I said to the sea, 'You may come
this far, but no farther; this is where your proud waves must stop'?"

JOB 38:1, 8–11

THE BEACH IS ONE OF MY FAVORITE PLACES to go and chill for a few days. There's just something healing about it. The sand, the waves, dolphins jumping up in the water—that is, if you get lucky enough to see them. And sea- gulls. Even though seagulls try to steal my food, I have actually found a new love for them, because Honey is convinced that each of them is Scuttle from *The Little Mermaid*. All to say, I love today's verses in Job 38 because they send me right back there—toes in the sand, waves crashing on the shore, which is a beautiful reminder of God's incredible power and authority over all of creation.

Genesis tells us that God created the heavens and the earth out of nothing. It was all formless and empty and dark, so He invented light. The second day was the sky; the third day the land, sea, and vegetation; the fourth day was the sun, moon, and stars; the fifth day fish and birds; and finally the sixth day animals and man. Even though you've likely heard or read those details hundreds of times, take

Thank You, God, for being the Lord over all. I am in awe of Your work—from the peaks to the oceans, from snowcapped mountains to the meadows of colorful wildflowers, along with the sun, moon, and stars that hold it all together. Thank You for creating people, for making me, and for entrusting this beautiful world to us. Today I declare Your glory and sovereignty over it all and promise to honor You with all I say and do—whether things go my way or not. Amen.

a minute to think about the enormity of what was done. God created the earth and everything in it for us. *For us!*

Visualizing the immense, miraculous event we call creation makes it a little easier to understand why God, in His greatness, humbled Job with His "Where were you when I did all of this?" response. Why was this important for Job to hear, and why does it matter to us today? Maybe because we need to recognize God's supreme sovereignty—that He's in charge, and we are not.

If you have ever noticed, my mom and I both have little wave tattoos on our arms. The inspiration behind these comes from Jeremiah 5:22: "'Should you not fear me?' declares the LORD. 'Should you not tremble in my presence? I made the sand a boundary for the sea, an everlasting barrier it cannot cross. The waves may roll, but they cannot prevail; they may roar, but they cannot cross it'" (NIV). When I'm sitting on the sandy beach and have this verse in my mind, it all blows me away.

A lot of things may happen to us that don't seem fair—relationship issues, diseases, loss of loved ones, job layoffs—things that bring us to our knees, overwhelm us with questions, and make us feel broken, angry, and sad. Though there aren't any quick fixes or easy answers, there is always God and His Word, which promises us two amazing things: one, He's got the whole world in His hands (Psalm 24:1); and two, He loves us and will never leave us or forsake us (Deuteronomy 31:8). The waves of life may roar and roll, but they will not prevail.

I hope, my sister and friend, that this gives you comfort. Our life and this world are not random. The Great Creator, who put it all together, still holds what He made in the palm of His almighty hands. And He always makes a way for us, through whatever storm we might be facing.

The next time you stand by the sea, remember the Creator of everything sees you, knows you, loves you, and has a beautiful plan for your life.

Find Your WAY

Every once in a while, it's good to zoom out and recognize how much bigger life is than all of the details going on in our individual worlds. Spend a few minutes outside today, noticing the beautiful creation all around you. Make a verbal list of all you observe, and then take a deep breath and say, "Thank You." When hard things come your way, remember that God has an intentional plan for your good and His glory. Nothing is random. Choose to see Him and seek Him always, and remember to thank Him.

Wisdom DAY 17

WE CAN ALL LEARN SOMETHING

Then Job answered the Lord: *"I know that you can do all things and that no plan of yours can be ruined. You asked, 'Who is this that made my purpose unclear by saying things that are not true?' Surely I spoke of things I did not understand; I talked of things too wonderful for me to know. You said, 'Listen now, and I will speak. I will ask you questions, and you must answer me.' My ears had heard of you before, but now my eyes have seen you."*

JOB 42:1–5

I'VE BEEN A PUBLIC SPEAKER NOW for close to a decade, but sometimes when I walk on stage, it still feels like the first time. I don't have it all figured out. Recently, I attended a conference for preachers and speakers designed to sharpen their craft of communicating the gospel, and I came home with seven pages of notes! I still have so much to learn.

Even if we aren't in the classroom anymore, it's important that we live as students, embracing a teachable spirit no matter what we do or how old we are. Our generation seems to be easily offended. Sometimes that means when someone older than us points out a place where we could grow, we're not super open to listening to feedback. It's definitely hard and humbling to start at the bottom, to hear how much you don't know, and to learn at the feet of superiors, but it's important to realize that all of life is a learning experience. In Job 12:12, we read: "Older people are wise, and long life brings understanding." And even among the oldest humans on earth, no one ever arrives at a place of knowing it *all*.

Job was a wealthy man who had ten children, many servants, and livestock that numbered into the thousands. He was also known as the greatest man among the people living around him at that time. When Satan asked God if he could pick on Job, it seemed like it was time for Job to learn a few things. How did Job respond? Our verses for today tell us that he acknowledged he didn't know it all. His response to God was, "I know that you can do all things and that no plan of Yours can be ruined" (Job 42:2).

The book of Job reminds us that we can all learn something—even the oldest,

Find Your WAY

Reading the book of Proverbs has helped me be a lifelong learner. This book offers us wisdom for living a godly life. Christian and I read through Proverbs together before we started dating, and I think it really helped us build a solid foundation for our relationship! With thirty-one chapters, it's perfect to read through in a month—one chapter a day, with the chapter number corresponding to the date. Try it for one month, and see if it sheds some light on your life.

wisest, and greatest among us. I love having mentors to learn from. Something I've noticed is that they will often lean in to also learn from me—a true reflection of their humility, especially when they know so much more than I do! But honestly, I learn so much from my daughters, and one of them can't even speak yet! I truly believe great leaders are those who always continue to learn.

Make a commitment to yourself to never think you are too good to learn from others. Stay humble and determined to become a forever-learner and a better student of life.

Lord, I really struggle with the insecurity that others are further along than I am. When I feel offended, help me to remember that no one knows it all—everyone has something to learn, and I want to be one of the teachable ones. Help me to be open to correction, to remember I can always learn something new or something more, and to understand that being wrong or receiving correction is not necessarily a personal attack. Only You are perfect, and You can help us become more like You. Amen.

Wisdom DAY 18

THE EBB AND FLOW OF FORGIVENESS

After Job had prayed for his friends, the Lord *gave him success again.*
The Lord *gave Job twice as much as he had owned before.*

JOB 42:10

I'VE SHARED BEFORE THAT WHEN I LEFT *Dancing with the Stars*, I had one million followers on social media but not a lot of friends in real life. It felt like many of the people I knew suddenly didn't want anything to do with me. It was one of the hardest and loneliest times of my life.

It also made my junior-senior prom very awkward. There was a comedian at prom that night who made a joke about me being on the show. Sitting in the crowd, in the middle of everyone, it was painfully obvious that not one person laughed. It was one of the most uncomfortable experiences of my life! The dude made it worse by quickly saying, "Oh, whoa. Okay, that's a touchy subject!" Yes, he really said that out loud.

My mom's dad, 2Papa, explained to me the social phenomenon Tall Poppy Syndrome. Visualize a field of poppy flowers. It looks best when all the flowers are the same height. When one grows taller than the others, the farmer chops it down so it doesn't stick out. The same can happen with people. Sometimes a success or accomplishment can make you stick out and become the target of criticism and gossip. It can be especially challenging if you're young and still building your confidence and competence, making you more likely to struggle with feelings of insecurity or envy.[1]

Job struggled in his relationship with his friends because they didn't understand what he was going through. When he began experiencing intense suffering, three of them came to offer advice and support. They knew God is just and decided that Job must have done something very wrong to bring that kind of trouble upon himself—and they told him so. In response, Job kept declaring his innocence, angry words were exchanged between the friends, and then God showed up. God declared that Job's friends were wrong—their understanding of the situation was too simple and just wasn't true, and He asked Job to pray for them. I can imagine Job thinking, *Whaaat? I'm supposed to pray for the friends who hurt me? For the people who spoke against me?*

This is not an easy thing—for us or for Job, especially in light of his suffering. But by God's grace, he forgave his friends. And did you notice that after Job prayed for his friends, the Lord gave him success again?

We have to let things go and forgive those who have hurt us. It takes courage and grace, and it can be *very* hard, but forgiveness helps us to move forward. I have found over the years that praying for people who hurt me has become a lot more natural too! It frees me from clinging to old baggage, and it heals my current relationships while preparing me for new ones.

Sometimes we find ourselves on the other side of the story, where we've been the unkind friend. No matter what side we're on, let's strive to be the type of believers who ask God to give us insight and are willing to humbly own our part of the conflict. That way, we can exist on both sides of the beautiful ebb and flow of forgiveness.

Father God, I have been hurt. Maybe it was intentional or maybe it wasn't, but the pain is the same either way. Please give me eyes to see what You have for me in this. Also give me the strength to let the situation go, to give it to You and trust that You have a plan. I know I need to forgive and that I can't do it on my own. Please help me as I pray the prayer You modeled for us in Matthew 6:9–13: "Our Father in heaven, may your name always be kept holy. May your kingdom come and what you want be done, here on earth as it is in heaven. Give us the food we need for each day. Forgive us for our sins, just as we have forgiven those who sinned against us. And do not cause us to be tempted, but save us from the Evil One. The kingdom, the power, and the glory are yours forever. Amen."

Find Your WAY

Are there hurts and hard feelings between you and someone else? Or maybe even several someones? If so, try to put what you're feeling into words. Write it all down on a piece of paper, and take it before the Lord. Pray and ask Him to help you forgive any offense. Then, take the paper outside. Burn it or shred it, and let the wind carry it away. Thank God for His miracle, knowing that forgiveness is actually more for you than it is for the other person!

Wisdom DAY 19

WHEN THINGS GET TOUGH

*The L*ORD* blessed the last part of Job's life even more than the first part.*

JOB 42:12

NICK VUJICIC IS LIVING PROOF that God can use a man born without arms and legs to be His hands and feet in the world. There was no medical reason for Nick's birth defects; in fact, his brother and sister born after him have no disabilities. Because he grew up being loved by his family and church community, it wasn't until he went to school and experienced bullying that he learned his disabilities were a big deal. From ages eight to twelve, Nick was severely depressed and felt as though he'd never be able to be independent, get a job, or get married. At age ten he attempted suicide. The only thing that stopped him was realizing he would be putting his parents into even more pain. How did he come out of his dark circumstances?

Even without arms and legs, Nick was a soccer player. A three-week period of time when he was laid up from a soccer injury helped him realize he needed to be thankful for what he *did* have. Then, at the age of fifteen, Nick was transformed by reading the story of the blind man in John 9—not because Jesus healed him, but because the man didn't ask any questions. Nick realized that whether God healed him or not, whether he did or didn't get that miracle, he could still *be* a miracle, since the greatest miracle of all is God's love and salvation. Giving his heart

**JESUS ANSWERED,
"IT IS NOT THIS MAN'S SIN
OR HIS PARENTS' SIN
THAT MADE HIM BLIND.
THIS MAN WAS BORN BLIND
SO THAT GOD'S POWER
COULD BE SHOWN IN HIM."**

John 9:3

Find Your WAY

Even though Nick can't physically hold her hand, he has been married to his wife Kanae for twelve years. Together they have four biological children. With a small foot that has two toes, Nick is mobile, can type fifty-three words a minute, swim, play soccer, surf, and even golf. He says when you put *go* in front of the word *disabled*, it becomes "God is able!" Nick's mission through his organization, Life Without Limbs, is to share the gospel with as many people as possible. The next time you want to tap out because whatever you're facing seems too hard, start counting your blessings, naming them one by one, and remember that Christ didn't call us to an easy life—He called us to love God, love others, and share the good news with everyone! As the incredible writer and speaker Katherine Wolfe said, "You have a stunning capacity to do really hard things." You never know what blessings He might have coming around the bend for you. Do not lose hope, friends!

and life to Jesus—and being transformed from being angry to being thankful—was the turning point in Nick's life.

Not naturally a positive, glass-half-full kind of guy, Nick, now forty years of age, went through depression again a few years ago. But he continues to work through his struggles with the Lord. He was taught that you don't know what you can achieve until you try. He also understands that you don't know what God can do until you hand over what you have to Him and walk by faith, not by sight.[1]

As believers in Christ, let's not tap out when life gets hard. Everyone in the Bible struggled, even Job whom God called a righteous man. It's not like you come to a point in your life when you've got it all figured out. It's an ongoing battle—especially when you do ministry. Like Nick said, "When you stand in front of the gates of hell and redirect traffic, it gets hot."[2] Those are the times when we can lean into the spirit of God that's inside of us. That's what Job and my friend Nick did when things got tough, and that's what we can ask God to help us do too.

Father, when things are tough, instead of complaining, help me to lean into the words of Isaiah 41:10: "So don't worry, because I am with you. Don't be afraid, because I am your God. I will make you strong and will help you; I will support you with my right hand that saves you." Thank You for Your promises that are always true. Thank You for helping me when things get tough. Amen.

Wisdom DAY 20

WHEN YOU DON'T FEEL SO GREAT

After this, Job lived one hundred forty years. He lived to see his children, grandchildren, great-grandchildren and great-great-grandchildren. Then Job died; he was old and had lived many years.

JOB 42:16–17

BEFORE WE LEAVE THE BOOK OF JOB this week, I want us to remember why it's such an important part of the Bible. As one of the oldest biblical writings, it's considered part of the Bible section people call the "wisdom literature," because the book gives critical insight into some of life's biggest questions: Why do good people have to suffer? Why does God allow it? And does He even care? I don't have all the answers, but when I look at the book of Job, I see how God is present. All-powerful. And still always good—even when things are not. I have no idea what you may be facing today, but I pray that no matter what, you know the presence and goodness of God.

With those truths in mind, let's talk more about Job. This is the guy who had everything taken away from him—his livelihood, his possessions, even his children. Then he was attacked physically and hit with painful sores from the bottom of his feet to the top of his head. His wife told him it was time to curse God and die. It was a no-good, very bad time for Job.

I don't know what it's like to deal with what Job experienced or to suffer from a long-term illness, but I've had a glimpse of how terrifying it can be when you get sick and your body seems to be failing you.

In 2020 I got COVID when I was pregnant with Honey. Still suffering from morning sickness, I was so ill that I was admitted into the hospital. First baby. First time dealing with a disease caused by a worldwide pandemic. And first time in the hospital by myself. I have to admit I was scared. And because the disease was so contagious, I also experienced the isolation and loneliness that COVID patients had to experience. I was by myself in the hospital, worried about my baby, and worried about the state of the world. It all felt so overwhelming.

What do you do when you just want to pull the covers over your head and make the world, and everything bad in it, go away? In that moment, I had no one to turn but to Jesus, who was right there waiting on me. My dependency on Him never felt greater than it did in those moments. Since that time I have continued to learn how to lean into God during times of suffering. God warned us that we would face trials, and that bad things happen because we live in a broken world. I'm so gratful He also said that He has overcome the world.

One thing I want to hold on to from the book of Job is that no matter what is happening, I want to stay the course with God like Job did. Will you join me? If you are currently struggling, then you may feel encouraged by this short exercise. Take a few quiet moments to review a few of God's names that describe His character:

El Shaddai—God Almighty
Abba—Father
Jehovah Ro'i—The Lord is our Shepherd
Jehovah Rapha—The Lord who heals
Jehovah Jireh—The Lord will provide
Jehovah Shalom—The Lord is peace
El Roi—The God who sees

You can trust that God does see, that He does provide, that He is the Almighty One—our Father, the Good Shepherd, that He brings peace, and that He heals.

Find Your WAY

If you are experiencing physical challenges, know that you're not alone. If you're not currently sick but know someone who is, consider taking them a meal, sending an inexpensive "I love you and I'm praying for you" gift, or running an errand for them. Your loving actions will make both of you feel better!

Lord, during our time here on earth, I know we aren't promised to experience all sunshine and no pain or sickness. So when those things come, help me keep my eyes on You. Thank You for always being our heavenly Father who knows and sees and provides and heals our every disease, in Your time and in Your way. Help me to always trust You. Thank You. Amen.

REFLECT on IT

As you reflect on the week, consider what you've learned about finding your way to the life God has mapped out for you. Highlight the statement(s) below that speak to you, then on the journaling lines write notes to yourself so you can remember God's truth and live it out every day.

- Remember that God, the Great Creator who brought the world into order, is in control, and we are not.

- Embrace a teachable spirit, and don't be easily offended; everyone has something they need to learn.

- Forgiving someone for an offense may seem impossible until you realize it's actually a gift you give to yourself.

- Don't tap out when things get hard. Instead, lean on God, knowing that together you are tougher than you think.

- Being physically ill can be challenging—scary, even—but God promises He will be with us through it all and that we can trust Him to provide whatever we need.

_____

_____

_____

REST and WORSHIP

God designed each week to include a day of rest. Use this day to take a time-out from the world and worship Him.

I've found that music is a gift that connects our spirits with God's Holy Spirit, whether we're listening to worship music that turns thoughts toward God, or we hear a song that describes exactly how we're feeling. Here are two of my favorites for this week:

- "There Was Jesus," by Zach Williams and Dolly Parton

- "Even If," by MercyMe

Thank You, Father, for the wisdom from Job. On the days I get ahead of myself, help me to remember that You are in control and I can trust You no matter what is going on around or even in me. I'm eager to hear from You again next week as we dig into some verses from Psalms. I love You. Amen.

5

God, be merciful to me because you are loving. Because you are always ready to be merciful, wipe out all my wrongs. Wash away all my guilt and make me clean again.

I know about my wrongs, and I can't forget my sin. You are the only one I have sinned against; I have done what you say is wrong. You are right when you speak and fair when you judge. I was brought into this world in sin. In sin my mother gave birth to me.

You want me to be completely truthful, so teach me wisdom. Take away my sin, and I will be clean. Wash me, and I will be whiter than snow. Make me hear sounds of joy and gladness; let the bones you crushed be happy again. Turn your face from my sins and wipe out all my guilt.

Create in me a pure heart, God, and make my spirit right again. Do not send me away from you or take your Holy Spirit away from me. Give me back the joy of your salvation. Keep me strong by giving me a willing spirit. Then I will teach your ways to those who do wrong, and sinners will turn back to you.

God, save me from the guilt of murder, God of my salvation, and I will sing about your goodness. Lord, let me speak so I may praise you. You are not pleased by sacrifices, or I would give them. You don't want burnt offerings. The sacrifice God wants is a broken spirit. God, you will not reject a heart that is broken and sorry for sin.

Do whatever good you wish for Jerusalem. Rebuild the walls of Jerusalem. Then you will be pleased with right sacrifices and whole burnt offerings, and bulls will be offered on your altar.

PSALM 51

Wisdom DAY 21

THE ALMOST-CHRISTIAN

God, be merciful to me because you are loving. Because you are
always ready to be merciful, wipe out all my wrongs.

PSALM 51:1

FOR THOUSANDS OF YEARS people all over the world have lived by a code of ethics that mirrors the teachings of God—*don't kill, lie, cheat, or steal; be kind to the poor; follow the Golden Rule*—without actually knowing God as their Lord and Savior. Even today, many fall into the trap of believing that because they know God's name, live a semi-moral life, and attend church, they have secured their ticket to heaven. But friend, God doesn't want you to just know *about* Him—He wants you to truly *know* Him. He doesn't want you to try to do the right thing on your own—He wants you to live a life empowered by His Spirit.

I see this everywhere I go: people identify themselves as Christians but they live in ways that aren't marked by Christ—not even in the smallest things. We certainly see this played out on social media. There may be a Bible verse in the bio, but the feed doesn't look anything like it. You may even be that person. If so, friend, I want to challenge you to really understand who God is and what it means to follow Him. If you only know *about* Him, there's so much you'll miss out on—the peace of mind, the strength, the wisdom, the hope, and the blessings that come from knowing Him.

My prayer is that this book helps you change the way you live as a Christ follower, and that it helps make your life better in every way. But my biggest hope for you? That you'll find your life *in* Christ. Because He makes all things new!

Maybe you're wondering how you can become a Christian. A true follower of Christ. It's really easy—repent from your old ways of living. Ask Jesus for forgiveness of your sins and sin nature. Thank Him for what He did for you on the cross.

Thank You, Jesus, for dying on the cross for me. For taking on the sin of the world—past, present, and future—and giving up Your own life as the ultimate sacrifice to pay for my sins. I pledge my allegiance to You and You alone. Each day, draw me closer to You. Amen.

Find Your WAY

If you have sincerely prayed, asking God to forgive you of your sins and inviting Jesus and His Holy Spirit into your life, then you are a follower of Christ. Being a Christ follower doesn't mean now you're perfect and you'll never sin again, but it *does* mean you are covered by God's grace and mercy as you become more like Him day by day. If you haven't prayed this prayer, please consider doing so, because being an almost-Christian is not being a Christian at all. There is no state of being "almost" Christian, just like there is no state of being "almost" alive or "almost" dead. You are one or the other.

Express belief in who He is and what He did for you. Then confess your belief in Him. From there you can become a brand-new person in Christ!

Think of it this way. Just like Christ died on the cross and came back to life, you are letting your sin die on that cross *with* Him to come back brand-new. From there you are sent back into the world with a clean slate—because all wrongs have been wiped out—to live your life in obedience to God and His Word. But God doesn't send you out alone. He puts His Holy Spirit in you to go with you and help you. You also have His guidebook, the Bible, to give you wisdom.

What does it look like to be marked by Christ? It can be summed up in two qualifying statements that come from Matthew 22:37–40:

1. A genuine Christian has a genuine love of God.
2. A genuine Christian has a genuine love of their neighbor.

God is love. And He's here now, extending the free gift of mercy and grace to you—a gift that, if you accept it, all of the wrong of your past, present, and future will be wiped out. Of that you can be sure!

Wisdom DAY 22

A GROWING FAITH

Wash away all my guilt and make me clean again. I know about my wrongs, and I can't forget my sin. You are the only one I have sinned against; I have done what you say is wrong. You are right when you speak and fair when you judge. I was brought into this world in sin. In sin my mother gave birth to me. You want me to be completely truthful, so teach me wisdom. Take away my sin, and I will be clean. Wash me, and I will be whiter than snow. Make me hear sounds of joy and gladness; let the bones you crushed be happy again. Turn your face from my sins and wipe out all my guilt.

PSALM 51:2–9

EVERYONE I KNOW WHO'S JUST COME to faith in Jesus is eager to start their new life with a clean slate, with the bone-crushing weight of past sin and guilt gone. They feel renewed and are ready to learn as they read God's Word and pray for wisdom to know how to live each day. I've found it's important to be surrounded by like-minded believers, so I encourage these people to look for a church to attend or a Bible study group to join.

As a new believer, when you find a place where you belong and begin to experience life with new friends who also believe, it's an amazing experience. Like a gift! Like you're home. All good . . . except home is also where the comfy recliner is that sits in front of the TV. As you settle into the new routine, it's easy to begin to relax. *I made it!* you might think. You attend a conference and get

Thank You, Jesus, for the Holy Spirit that lives in me to guide me and help me every single day. Open my eyes and help me see where You are calling me to serve You. And give me a willing spirit to sustain me when it all gets hard. I don't want to live my life halfway but instead fully devoted to You. In Your name I pray, amen.

excited about serving God, but then you go home and get dulled into complacency because, well, life is busy. Understood. Maybe next time.

The only problem is that next time never really comes around—it's always in the future.

To grow any relationship, we must make it a daily priority. The same is true with your faith in God. You don't grow when you just spend time with others worshiping God on Sunday morning. Making sure your faith stays strong means that faith needs to be alive and active Monday, Tuesday, Wednesday, Thursday, Friday,

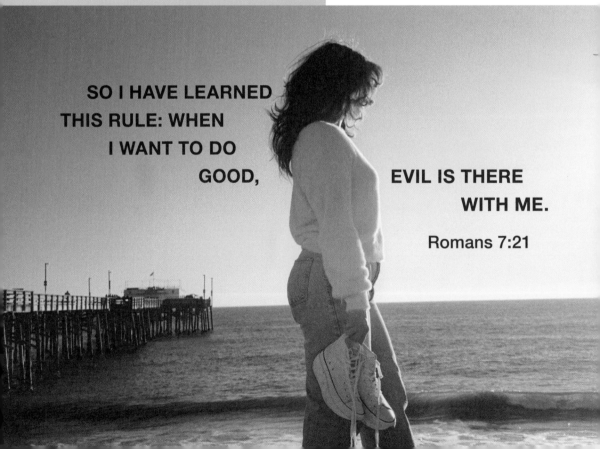

SO I HAVE LEARNED THIS RULE: WHEN I WANT TO DO GOOD, EVIL IS THERE WITH ME.

Romans 7:21

Saturday, *and* Sunday, with your beliefs showing up in your words, your thoughts, and your deeds.

Easy? Not quite. We have an Enemy who causes us to struggle and even stumble. To get distracted by the things of this world. In Romans 7:7–25, Paul shared his fight against sin and the ongoing war within, explaining how we all have the capacity to sin every day. We are in-process people, but if we're not moving forward, we're actually moving backward. If everything in life is in motion—and it is—then our faith should be too. The beautiful thing is that the more you walk with God, the more naturally you will walk as a child of His. I'm reading a book right now called *You Are What You Love*, by James K. A. Smith. The whole point of it is that it's not what you know that changes you, it's what you love. And as day by day you fall more and more in love with God, that love will reshape your wants, desires, and habits.

Our verses for today remind us of our past and how God has washed us clean from it. What should our response to Him be? Ask Him for wisdom about how to live with gratefulness, but also how to fulfill the call to love Him, love our neighbor, and share the Good News. Often that is done through both serving others and actively seeking and spending time with God. It requires that we get up out of the recliner, go beyond the front door of our houses and churches, and be Jesus to everyone we meet . . . every day of the week.

Find Your WAY

Think back to a conference, church, or faith-related gathering you've attended in the past. Now ask God to remind you of a seed He may have planted in you around a growth area or a service to Him. If you can't find any of these seeds, make this a specific matter of prayer, then keep your eyes and ears open. Since we're supposed to be God's hands and feet in this world, there's no doubt He wants to use you. Don't be afraid that He's going to call you to something you wouldn't love. Since He's the One who created you, He knows you and knows what fits you. Maybe not the exact *you* that you are today, but the you that you'll love being tomorrow.

Wisdom DAY 23

THIS HOUSE WILL SET THE TONE

Create in me a pure heart, God, and make my spirit right again. Do not send me away from you or take your Holy Spirit away from me. Give me back the joy of your salvation. Keep me strong by giving me a willing spirit. Then I will teach your ways to those who do wrong, and sinners will turn back to you.

PSALM 51:10–13

WHEN CHRISTIAN AND I COOKED our first meal together as a newlywed couple, we talked about our life and how we wanted to live it. We wanted our years on earth to reflect what God had given us with pure hearts, joy, and willing spirits to follow Him in every area of our lives. During our conversation we found ourselves repeating the phrase, "This house will set the tone." What we meant was that what happens inside our house—our home—will determine what we do outside of it.

We've come to realize that living this out is not a one-time decision, but something we choose over and over again. To intentionally set up our home so that our actions inside and outside it bring joy, connection, and peace. To create both a place and a set of practices that will help each member of our family greet the day saying, "Create in me a pure heart, God. Give me the joy of Your salvation and a willing spirit."

Find Your WAY

Have you ever realized that your space reflects your life? More than a place to lay your head, your home is where you feed your body and your soul. It truly sets the tone for your life. So take time this week to think about this. Maybe walk through the rooms with the people who share the space with you—your roommate, your spouse, your kids— and talk about how your physical place sets the tone for the life you live together. It is amazing how being intentional about your space can change the way you feel inside it, and how others feel when they're invited in. There's nothing like feeling—and sharing— peace in your home.

Setting the tone of your home begins with intentionality, even in the small things: choose to connect with your spouse by holding hands instead of holding your phone. Talk about serving each other by trading out the not-so-fun jobs—like who takes out the trash or cleans up the spills in the refrigerator. And now that we have children, making these choices has become even more important, because we are also setting the tone for our kids' lives.

But no matter where you live—an apartment, a dorm, a room in someone else's house—you can still begin practicing intentionality. It will absolutely set the tone for so many parts of your life not just today, but for all of your tomorrows.

Father, create in me a pure heart, and make my spirit right with Yours. Give me joy, strength, and a willing spirit to live my life in a way that honors You. Thank You for giving me a place to call home. Please help me to establish it both visually and purposely to honor and reflect You. Amen.

Wisdom DAY 24

A BROKEN, CONTRITE HEART

God, save me from the guilt of murder, God of my salvation, and I will sing about your goodness. Lord, let me speak so I may praise you. You are not pleased by sacrifices, or I would give them. You don't want burnt offerings. The sacrifice God wants is a broken spirit. God, you will not reject a heart that is broken and sorry for sin.

PSALM 51:14–17

IS IT POSSIBLE TO BE KNOWN as a "man after God's own heart" when you are also remembered as one of history's most well-known sinners? Enter King David. He wrote Psalm 51 after he committed adultery with Bathsheba and had her husband murdered.

How did David get to such a low point? And how could he ever again be used by God?

David was first anointed by God when he was a young shepherd boy. At the time he wasn't from a big city, he wasn't out promoting himself, and he wasn't striving to make his way to the palace so that someday he could be king. He was simply keeping the sheep, playing his music, and living faithfully. It didn't matter where he was—David's concern was being where God had called him to be, which was out in the fields tending sheep.

It also didn't matter what possessions David had. When it came time to fight Goliath the giant, all David had was his shepherd's staff, a slingshot, and five

Father, I know I'm a sinner saved only by Your grace. And though my desire is to follow You perfectly, I'm also admitting that I mess up. I recognize that because I'm human, I will most likely continue to make poor choices along the way. Through it all, help me to stay open, humble, and honest before You. Thank You for Your mercies, which are new every morning. Great is Your faithfulness! Amen.

stones he'd picked up from a nearby stream. David knew he also had God on his side, and so he confidently went into battle to slay the giant.

But David was not perfect or perfectly obedient. He was human. When God sent the prophet Nathan to confront David with his sin against Bathsheba and her husband Uriah, David came to God with great humility and a sincere prayer of confession and repentance. It's why he began Psalm 51 with, "God, be merciful to

HE SAID TO ME, "MY GRACE IS ENOUGH FOR YOU. WHEN YOU ARE WEAK, MY POWER IS MADE PERFECT IN YOU." SO I AM VERY HAPPY TO BRAG ABOUT MY WEAKNESSES. THEN CHRIST'S POWER CAN LIVE IN ME.

2 Corinthians 12:9

me. . . . Wash away all my guilt and make me clean again."

Scripture reminds us that no one is sinless, except the Lord Jesus Christ. All of us will make mistakes. All of us will mess up. And all of us will be held accountable for our actions. But where there is humility and repentance, there is also grace. God simply wants us to come to Him and confess our sins. And when we do, He doesn't ask us to repeat a certain number of prayers or give money to a charity. God is a relational God. The key to experiencing His forgiveness is a pure heart before Him, a true moment of repentence. There will always be consequences to our actions, but as our verse today reminds us, God will never reject a heart that is broken and sorry for sin. Receive His grace today.

Find Your WAY

Think back through your life, and identify a couple times you made a wrong choice. And though there are consequences for our choices, consider how God's grace allowed you to be forgiven and move on. If you have recently become aware of an ongoing sin issue, don't wait another minute! Turn to the Lord now and ask Him to forgive you, to wash away your guilt and make you clean again. If you've wronged someone, ask God how you can make it right between you and that person. Making amends may be hard, and things may not be like they were before, but God will honor your humility with His peace and His presence.

Wisdom DAY 25

GOD REBUILDS US

Do whatever good you wish for Jerusalem. Rebuild the walls of Jerusalem. Then you will be pleased with right sacrifices and whole burnt offerings, and bulls will be offered on your altar.

PSALM 51:18–19

ONE OF THE HARDEST THINGS for any kid to understand is the phrase, "I'm disciplining you because I love you." But now that Christian and I are parents, we're leaning into those words as we parent our girls.

For instance, when Honey deliberately disobeys rules we've put in place to keep her safe or healthy, we respond with discipline designed to help her learn how to be obedient. Why is that important? Because ignoring Honey's moments of rebellion is a total disservice to her. Sin has consequences that cause suffering of some kind or another. And the sooner she learns that hard lesson, the better her life will be.

One thing I've noticed is that even when we're disciplining her, and she's crying because of the consquences of her rebellion, Honey still wants me to hold her, and I do. I want her to see that even when she messes up, I love her and want what's best for her.

I used to think that conviction was a bad thing—you know, that feeling when you *know* you're wrong. I hated feeling convicted, but Christian helped me understand that conviction is a gift from the Holy Spirit. It is so good to know that God convicts me of my sin so I won't want to continue living in it, and so that I will be brought to repentance.

That's where King David found himself. Loved but severely disciplined and convicted after he took Bathsheba into his palace to sleep with her and then had her husband killed. What was the consequence of David's sins? The Lord told David that though he'd acted in secret, his consequences would be seen by the whole country. David and Bathsheba lost their first child, and more tragedy would plague the family in the future.

> Father, Thank You for Your Word that includes stories of those with imperfect lives so that we can not only see Your plan for the world, but trace Your hand in how You work. Thank You for never giving up on me! Open my eyes to seeing Your work in my past so that together we can work on my future. Amen.

How are we supposed to weather horrible storms, whether we're the one who have willfully disobeyed or we're caught in the whirlwind that surrounds someone else's sinful choices? Pastor and author Chuck Swindoll looked into David's responses, and he pointed out a few helpful guidelines we can follow.

David's first response was prayer. He fell before God and lay on the ground all night long. He fasted and waited to hear from God. He made no demands but pled with God for the life of his child. During this time of waiting, he didn't bathe or change his clothes for seven days.[1]

David faced the consequences and continued to serve and worship God, even in the midst of tragedy. Though David's servants were afraid to tell him that his child had died, when he heard the news he quietly got up, bathed, changed his clothes, and went home to worship God.[2]

David claimed the truth of God's words and His ways. When crisis strikes, you can't let emotions be your guide. You need the truth and comfort

YOU ARE GOD'S CHILDREN WHOM
HE LOVES, SO TRY TO BE LIKE HIM.
LIVE A LIFE OF LOVE JUST AS
CHRIST LOVED US AND GAVE HIMSELF
FOR US AS A SWEET-SMELLING
OFFERING AND SACRIFICE TO GOD.

Ephesians 5:1–2

of God's counsel. This is what helped David accept the reality of the situation. Claiming the truth of God's Word brings amazing stability.[3]

Let's be sure that if we find ourselves being disciplined, or living in the aftermath of someone else's wrong choices, we remember David's response and accept that there will be consequences to sin. Also, remember that God has the authority to continue doing whatever He believes is best to rebuild us and those around us as each day we become more like Christ.

God is in the reconstruction business! He is rebuilding all of us day by day.

Find Your WAY

It's easy to become lulled into complacency, thinking what we do doesn't really matter since God will simply forgive us and we can move on. Not true! Paul said in Romans 6, "Are we to continue in sin that grace may abound? By no means!" (vv. 1–2 ESV). When we're found in Christ, we remain accountable to Him, which means there are consequences to our actions. To help you maintain boundaries that'll keep you from slipping into sin, consider sharing some of your vulnerabilities and struggles with your most trusted friend. Then check in with that friend every so often and share how you're doing. Holding yourself accountable in this way may save you from a poor choice down the road and remind you that you don't have to fight a tough battle alone.

REFLECT on IT

As you reflect on the week, consider what you've learned about finding your way to the life God has mapped out for you. Highlight the statement(s) below that speak to you, then on the journaling lines write notes to yourself so you can remember God's truth and live it out every day.

- God does not want you to just know *about* Him—He wants you to truly *know* Him.

- Grow in your faith every day, not just on Sunday.

- Be aware that your home environment and your daily practices set the tone for your life.

- When you become aware of sinful behaviors, stop what you're doing immediately and, with humility, ask God to forgive you.

- If you find yourself being disciplined by conviction, be grateful that God is continuing to work in your life, rebuilding you to make you more and more like Him.

_____

_____

_____

REST and WORSHIP

God designed each week to include a day of rest. Use this day to take a time-out from the world and worship Him. Whether it's worship music that helps us turn our eyes and thoughts toward God or a song that describes exactly how we're feeling, music is a gift that helps connect our spirit with God's Holy Spirit. Here are two of my favorites for this week:

- "Build My Life," by Housefires, featuring Pat Barrett

- "Open the Eyes of My Heart," by Michael W. Smith

Father, it's been a deeply introspective week reading through this Psalm of David's sin, broken heart, and repentance. I understand that it's not just a check-the-box, "I'm sorry, please forgive me" response that alleviates my guilt, but that I need to turn to You in true repentance and deal with my heart issues. In Jesus' name, amen.

6

Be generous: Invest in acts of charity. Charity yields high returns.

Don't hoard your goods; spread them around. Be a blessing to others. This could be your last night.

When the clouds are full of water, it rains. When the wind blows down a tree, it lies where it falls. Don't sit there watching the wind. Do your own work. Don't stare at the clouds. Get on with your life.

Just as you'll never understand the mystery of life forming in a pregnant woman, so you'll never understand the mystery at work in all that God does.

Go to work in the morning and stick to it until evening without watching the clock. You never know from moment to moment how your work will turn out in the end.

Oh, how sweet the light of day, and how wonderful to live in the sunshine! Even if you live a long time, don't take a single day for granted. Take delight in each light-filled hour, remembering that there will also be many dark days and that most of what comes your way is smoke.

You who are young, make the most of your youth. Relish your youthful vigor. Follow the impulses of your heart. If something looks good to you, pursue it. But know also that not just anything goes; you have to answer to God for every last bit of it.

Live footloose and fancy-free—you won't be young forever. Youth lasts about as long as smoke.

ECCLESIASTES 11 MSG

The last and final word is this: Fear God. Do what he tells you. And that's it. Eventually God will bring everything that we do out into the open and judge it according to its hidden intent, whether it's good or evil.

ECCLESIASTES 12:13–14 MSG

Wisdom DAY 26

WHATEVER YOU DO

Be generous: Invest in acts of charity. Charity yields high returns. Don't hoard your goods; spread them around. Be a blessing to others. This could be your last night.

ECCLESIASTES 11:1–2 MSG

THE BOOK OF ECCLESIASTES is Solomon's search for true meaning in life. He covers the pursuit of pleasure, work, possessions, even wisdom itself to find fulfillment. And what's his conclusion? That all pursuits and efforts—even the "good" ones—amount to nothing if they're done apart from centering our lives on God. This doesn't mean we're supposed to sit at home and do nothing—the point is that in whatever we do, we will only find purpose and satisfaction if we do it to serve and please God. Otherwise, our efforts are as meaningless as chasing the wind, a memorable description used six times in the book's twelve chapters.[1]

Do you, like me, ever have days where what you do seems meaningless? You put so much effort into something, and then, *poof!* It's over and done. Either it didn't work, you didn't get any praise, or nobody cared. Or maybe you're in a season where work itself doesn't seem to matter. You don't love it—it's hard, boring, or it feels below your pay grade. Some days really do feel like we're chasing the wind.

It's easy to get discouraged, which is why one of my favorite sermons is

"Passion, Purpose, and Designer Jeans" from pastor Louie Giglio. It's based on Colossians 3:23, which says, "In all the work you are doing, work the best you can. Work as if you were doing it for the Lord, not for people." Louie explained that it's not so much preachers and full-time ministry people who will win the world over to following Jesus; it's the daily interactions of Christian women and men living out their calling in the real world.[2] I loved when Julie Chen Moonves was on my podcast and we talked about a line she wrote in her book *But First, God* that really struck me: "There is no such thing as a secular job. Any job can be a job where you give glory to God."[3] Amen.

Our work, no matter what it is, *does* matter for growing God's kingdom. Whether you want to be a mom, an educator, a medical professional, or a maker of designer jeans, all of it fits into the "in all the work you are doing" idea. And it's key that we don't do that work half-heartedly. When we work the best we can as if doing it for the Lord, this then helps fulfill God's call on us to become more and more like His Son. Our work should be honorable; it should make us stand out from the crowd. It should show kindness and generosity to others—in other words, we should be a blessing no matter what we do or where we do it.

Some days are hard, sister. The work feels endless. But when we're seeking God and working for Him in whatever we do, not only can He give us joy and satisfaction in our work, He can use it for His good and His glory. He can use *us* and even the so-called meaningless tasks in our days to bless others and to help them see Him in us.

> Father, thank You for the wisdom to know how to serve You best in my everyday life. I want to be a light in a dark world. Help me shine for You in whatever I do. Amen.

Find Your WAY

We often think people find God through some big moment at church, a conference, or a retreat of some sort. Yes, they do, but more often they find Him when they see how God is changing *us*. It's important to minister at home—that's where our ministry needs to start, but then it should follow us into our neighborhoods and workplaces. And since it happens in our day-to-day living, whatever we do, consider how *you* can show God's love to those around you.

Wisdom DAY 27

LIVING OUT YOUR PASSIONS AND PURPOSE

When the clouds are full of water, it rains. When the wind blows down a tree, it lies where it falls. Don't sit there watching the wind. Do your own work. Don't stare at the clouds. Get on with your life. Just as you'll never understand the mystery of life forming in a pregnant woman, so you'll never understand the mystery at work in all that God does. Go to work in the morning and stick to it until evening without watching the clock. You never know from moment to moment how your work will turn out in the end.

ECCLESIASTES 11:3–6 MSG

WHEN I WAS A LITTLE GIRL, I would get up on our kitchen countertop and "preach" to my parents about the love of God. Who knew *that's* what I'd be doing when I grew up! Honestly, as a kid I had many other ideas of who I wanted to be. An Olympic gymnast was one, even though I couldn't do a cartwheel. There was also a time when I was obsessed with the weather and wanted to be a weather reporter. That career wasn't all I thought about, but it was my go-to response whenever an adult asked me what I wanted to do when I grew up. Looking back, it seems obvious what I would end up doing, considering the person I've always been. But my confidence had to mature, as did I.

Genesis is the story of the beginning of everything, of how God created the heavens and the earth. From the start He had a master plan for how it would all work together. In His love for us, He also had plans for how we needed to live and work as the caretakers of it all. We weren't created as blank slates—God wove individual passions (desires), purpose (a reason), and abilities (skills) into our beings so we could live out our uniqueness in relationship with Him and each other.

Our verses for today are clear about how we're supposed to live. There are many things we have no control over, so we shouldn't sit "watching the wind." I hear a lot of people use the term *waiting season*. But if we are not careful, our "waiting" can end up looking a lot more like "watching the wind" (v. 4).

Consider this: God has something for us to do even in the waiting! We need to pay attention to our responsibilities and do the work that's in front of us. And tomorrow? It's in God's hands. If we ask Him to direct us in living out the passions and the purpose He's placed inside us, we can trust He will do just that. He will lead us to open doors of possibility that we can then walk through. And as those passions become more alive, we will simultaneously be able to fulfill our purpose. And according to Scripture our purpose is to:

love God (Matthew 22:37)

love others (Matthew 22:39)

become like Christ (Philippians 2:5–11)

tell others about Him (Matthew 28:19–20)

do good works (Ephesians 2:10)

When you were a kid, maybe you weren't so sure about who you wanted to be and what you wanted to do. Maybe you're still not so sure. But never doubt that you were made with unique passions and created *on* purpose *with* a purpose in God's master plan. So get on with your life! There are some mysteries you'll never understand. Go to work in the morning, and stick with it until evening without watching the clock. After all, you never know from moment to moment how your work will turn out in the end.

Jesus, it can be so easy to get confused. Please help me keep my eyes on You and the work You've put in front of me today. Help me to love You, love others, become more like You and tell others about You, and continue to live and work for You as I put tomorrow in Your hands. Amen.

Find Your WAY
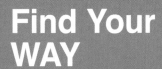

Waiting can be so challenging. I mean, think about it. Who likes a waiting room? Typically, a waiting room—like at a doctor's office—is where you do useless things as you wait your turn to be seen. Maybe you spend the time reading a magazine, scrolling your phone, looking at the clock, or getting frustrated that you've been waiting so long. The current season of your life might feel like that. You're not where you want to be, and it seems like a waste of time. But friend, there is not one season of your life that is a waste of time. Every era of your life has a purpose behind it. What God is doing in you right now will impact what He does through you later. Ask Him to change your perspective so you can see purpose in the places and spaces you're in right now.

Wisdom DAY 28

IT'S OKAY TO MESS UP

*Oh, how sweet the light of day, and how wonderful to live in the sunshine!
Even if you live a long time, don't take a single day for granted. Take
delight in each light-filled hour, remembering that there will also be
many dark days and that most of what comes your way is smoke.*

ECCLESIASTES 11:7–8 MSG

I WILL NEVER FORGET THE REVELATION I had when Christian and I moved into our first house. It all looked so perfect that honestly it felt too good to be true. And in some weird way I felt unworthy to live in it. Then I realized something very powerful—this house was now our home, the one place in the world I get to be fully me, and where all of my mess is truly welcome. It was mine not just to come into, but to live in. It was a beautiful picture of the truth that we belong to the house and the family of God, which sometimes seems too good to be true. We think we need to muster up perfection to really belong, until we realize that we have always been invited, just as we are.

As we were moving in, 2Papa gave us a cheesy-looking hammer that had words written on it about building a home together. He wanted us to hang it on the wall, but my grandma quickly jumped in and said it wasn't the kind of house where you hang just anything on the wall. I realized she was right: this was a home. Whatever we hung on our walls needed to have some meaning.

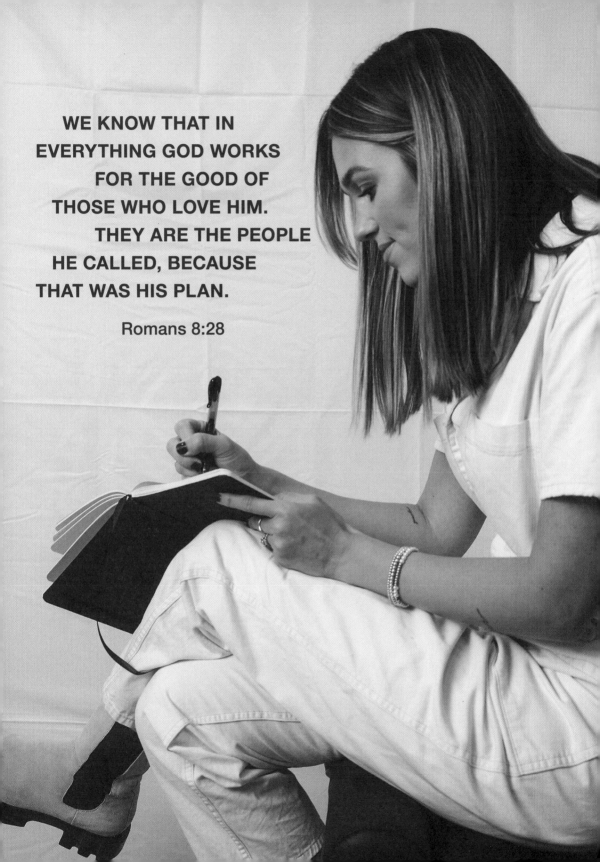

WE KNOW THAT IN
EVERYTHING GOD WORKS
FOR THE GOOD OF
THOSE WHO LOVE HIM.
THEY ARE THE PEOPLE
HE CALLED, BECAUSE
THAT WAS HIS PLAN.

Romans 8:28

Find Your WAY

Are you contanstly anxious that somehow you'll mess things up? Worry like this often comes from a misplaced fear of disappointing someone or simply embarrassing yourself. Ask God to open your eyes to the real reason for your concern, and then move forward accordingly.

While we ended up not hanging up the hammer, I did buy an inexpensive canvas and some paint to create something that would symbolize the tone we wanted to set for our home. I decided to paint out the lyrics to the song "Firm Foundation (He Won't)," by Cody Carnes, in my messy handwriting, because the words describe the kind of foundation I hope our family is building our lives on. Christian and I hung the canvas by our front door so that the minute people walk in, they'll know they're welcome, just as they are.

Sister, use whatever God has given you for His purposes. Don't be afraid to enjoy the gift, work the gift, and share the gift. Besides, your idea of "messing it up" is not God's. He uses everything—every single thing—for our good and His glory.

Lord, I know You not only have the whole world in Your hands, You also have my life. And for some reason You trust me, so help me learn to trust myself and not be afraid. Help me learn that I can't mess up Your plan if I'm following You. Help me to use the talents and opportunities You've given me to Your glory. Amen.

Wisdom DAY 29

YOU GET TO CHOOSE

You who are young, make the most of your youth. Relish your youthful vigor. Follow the impulses of your heart. If something looks good to you, pursue it. But know also that not just anything goes; you have to answer to God for every last bit of it. Live footloose and fancy-free— you won't be young forever. Youth lasts about as long as smoke.

ECCLESIASTES 11:9–10 MSG

I CAN'T DELETE IT. *I can't turn it off. I can't stop.*

Have you ever said this about something in your life? Comments like this often refer to social media and our online connection to the world around us, but this could apply to any activity we're engaged in—shopping, bingeing a show, eating . . . you name it!

We might say "I can't" about a lot of things, but the reality is that we get to be in control of what we believe, think, and do. We have the freedom to choose. And here's the thing: we need to choose well. Our verse today tells us that we need to make the most of our youth. Because as far as our earthly bodies go, they will not last forever. And for everything we do—or don't do—we will answer to God for every last bit.

So let's get back to our choices—specifically, back to the social media scenario. In recent years society's been talking a lot about the time we spend

Father, help me
to choose well as
You surround me
with Your wisdom
so that I can know
what I need to let
go of, what I need
to keep, and where
my focus needs
to be. Amen.

posting and scrolling, and the harmful effects it has on our physical and mental health. There are even reports that staying tethered to our phones and social apps is rewiring our brains to constantly crave instant gratification—not good.[1] Then there are the relationship issues that result from not being fully present when we're with friends and loved ones.

All of this is especially hard if you are an online influencer and feel it's essential to continue to provide content for your followers. I've certainly had those concerns—that is, until I realized I was trading a once-in-a-lifetime opportunity to be fully attentive to my girls while they're little for the sake of people I didn't even know. As a result, for a period

of time, I pulled back significantly from posting and have found incredible peace of mind. Is it worth it? For me, absolutely. Now, I'm not saying I haven't struggled. Even writing this devotional brings me a little anxiety because I am still right there with you, struggling to balance my time and focus.

What about your choices? Maybe you don't yet have a family, so you're choosing to focus more on your education. Perhaps you'd like to invest in yourself at your current job, or you're taking time to develop your friendships. Or maybe you need to simply slow down, focus more on God, and choose to take better care of your body, mind, and spirit. Again, it all comes down to choice. Remember, sister, it's not that we can't do something—it's that we get to choose what we do. And we need God's wisdom for both the big life choices and the small daily habits.

What an amazing thing to discover: that we get to choose! It comes with being an adult and being responsible for yourself. And though there will always be consequences to our actions (or inactions), when we factor in the truth today's Bible verse offers—that we won't live forever—we realize we're able to control what we do when we're alive. We get to choose!

Find Your WAY

Every cell phone can track how much time you spend on it. But screen time on your phone isn't the only thing that can steal away your time and focus. Ask God to help you become aware of where you're spending your time and energy, and to track how distractions are keeping you from doing what you really want to do. Consider making a list of things you wish you could (or should!) either limit or give up. I'm not trying to guilt trip you; I'm trying to help you become more aware of the choices you're making. Because everything in life *is* a choice.

Wisdom DAY 30

HOW GOD SEES US

The last and final word is this: Fear God. Do what he tells you. And that's it. Eventually God will bring everything that we do out into the open and judge it according to its hidden intent, whether it's good or evil.

ECCLESIASTES 12:13–14 MSG

AS THE MOM OF A TODDLER AND A BABY, I'm seeing life through new eyes—and to my precious little girls, everything is new and so much fun! The wonder of childhood certainly makes it easier for kids to be happy and carefree. In somewhat the same way, Ecclesiastes chapter eleven helps us to see that youth, though brief, is a time to enjoy life.

Chapter twelve takes it a step further, reminding us that these days don't last, but the text doesn't just leave it there. Solomon's final piece of advice in Ecclesiastes, which helps us better understand how to live this life of having faith and enjoying God's good gifts, is this: to fear God and to do what He tells us to do.

Don't let the word *fear* throw you. It's not saying to be afraid of God; instead, it means to respect Him. And if you do, if you've given your heart and life to Him, you'll want to do what He says because you understand that He is the way—the *only* way—to truth and life! It's no longer a power struggle—it's a transformational way to live. When we realize that as we submit ourselves to God, He in turn gives us everything we need to live. And living like this sets us free.

In this freedom, serving God and doing what He tells us to do doesn't feel like a heavy burden. Instead we feel encouraged to love and serve Him with joy because we have a greater understanding of how God sees us. He sees who we *really* are through the eyes of His love. Numerous verses remind us of His great and perfect love. Here are just a few:

- The Father has loved us so much that we are called children of God (1 John 3:1).
- Christ's love is greater than anyone can ever know, but I pray that you will be able to know that love. Then you can be filled with the fullness of God (Ephesians 3:19).
- Yes, I am sure that neither death, nor life, nor angels, nor ruling spirits, nothing now, nothing in the future, no powers, nothing above us, nothing below us, nor anything else in the whole world will ever be able to separate us from the love of God that is in Christ Jesus our Lord (Romans 8:38–39).

In today's verses we read that through the lens of His love, God sees everything—the good, the bad, and even the ugly things we thought were buried deep and out of sight. Much like a parent who you think doesn't know what you're *really* going through, He knows. He sees. And most importantly, He loves you no matter what you've done.

It's why John 3:16 is the ultimate love verse. It reminds us God sent Jesus, His only Son, to live as a man; to take on the sins of every person past, present, and future; to die a cruel death on a very cruel cross so that we would have a pathway to become clean and live with our Father in heaven for eternity.

We may no longer be kids, but we're always seen through His eyes of love and ultimate sacrifice. And that is enough to help us respect and follow Him all the days of our lives.

> Thank You, Father, for Your ultimate gift of love. I offer up my life to You again today to follow Your will and Your way. I am Yours. Amen.

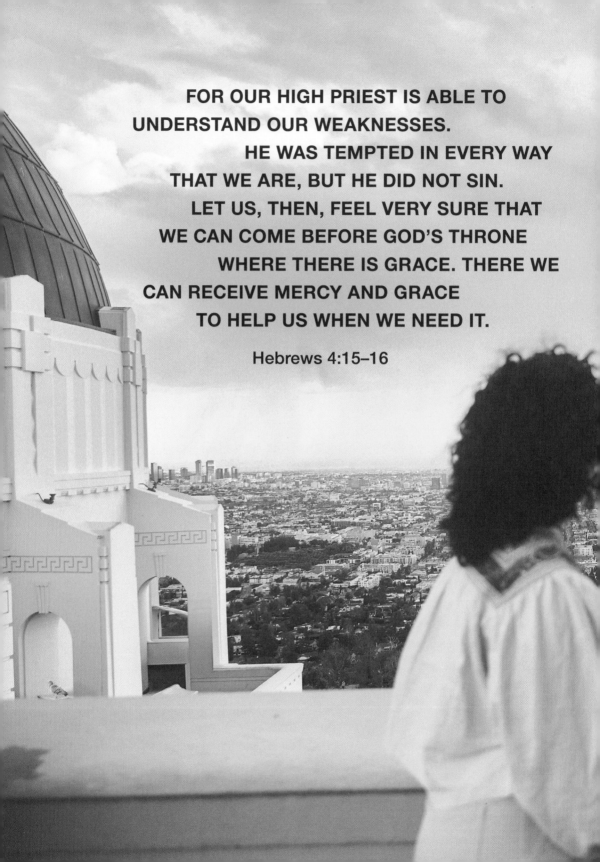

FOR OUR HIGH PRIEST IS ABLE TO UNDERSTAND OUR WEAKNESSES. HE WAS TEMPTED IN EVERY WAY THAT WE ARE, BUT HE DID NOT SIN. LET US, THEN, FEEL VERY SURE THAT WE CAN COME BEFORE GOD'S THRONE WHERE THERE IS GRACE. THERE WE CAN RECEIVE MERCY AND GRACE TO HELP US WHEN WE NEED IT.

Hebrews 4:15–16

Find Your WAY

Get real with how you feel about God saying that you are to follow Him and do what He tells you to do. Write down anything that comes to mind as a possible pushback or resentment. Is there a specific feeling you've been avoiding? Are you carrying guilt that continues to nag at you? If not, then thank God for where you are. But if something or someone comes to mind, then write about the situation and take it before God in prayer. Go back to the verses above that remind us of God's love, and highlight the words that speak to you. Remember, living is not about control as much as it is about being transformed. He loves you more than you could ever know!

REFLECT on IT

As you reflect on the week, consider what you've learned about finding your way to the life God has mapped out for you. Highlight the statement(s) below that speak to you, then on the journaling lines write notes to yourself so you can remember God's truth and live it out every day.

- The way we infiltrate the culture is to influence it by the way we live.

- Be faithful in your current responsibilities as you live out your purpose, which is to show Jesus to the world.

- Don't allow the fear of messing up keep you from using whatever God has given you.

- You have the power to choose what you do.

- Consider God's great love as you look to Him and follow Him all the days of your life.

_____

_____

_____

REST and WORSHIP

God designed each week to include a day of rest. Use this day to take a time-out from the world and worship Him. Whether it's worship music that helps us turn our eyes and thoughts toward God, or a song that describes exactly how we're feeling, music is a gift that helps connect our spirit with God's Holy Spirit. Here are two of my favorites for this week:

- "Firm Foundation (He Won't)," by Maverick City Music, featuring Chandler Moore and Cody Carnes

- "How He Loves," by David Crowder*Band

Lord, thank You for Ecclesiastes, the book that reminds me to not put too much focus on things that don't last. Instead, Jesus, I purposely put my eyes and my focus on You! Thank You for Your daily wisdom that helps me make the most of my life. Amen.

The Lord is your protection; you have made God Most High your place of safety. Nothing bad will happen to you; no disaster will come to your home. He has put his angels in charge of you to watch over you wherever you go. They will catch you in their hands so that you will not hit your foot on a rock. You will walk on lions and cobras; you will step on strong lions and snakes.

PSALM 91:9–13

It was good for me to be afflicted so that I might learn your decrees. The law from your mouth is more precious to me than thousands of pieces of silver and gold.

PSALM 119:71–72 NIV

Your word is like a lamp for my feet and a light for my path. I will do what I have promised and obey your fair laws.

PSALM 119:105–106

Children are a gift from the Lord; babies are a reward. Children who are born to a young man are like arrows in the hand of a warrior. Happy is the man who has his bag full of arrows. They will not be defeated when they fight their enemies at the city gate.

PSALM 127:3–5

You made my whole being; you formed me in my mother's body. I praise you because you made me in an amazing and wonderful way. What you have done is wonderful. I know this very well. You saw my bones being formed as I took shape in my mother's body. When I was put together there, you saw my body as it was formed. All the days planned for me were written in your book before I was one day old.

PSALM 139:13–16

Wisdom DAY 31

PEACE IN THE MIDST OF FEAR

The LORD is your protection; you have made God Most High your place of safety. Nothing bad will happen to you; no disaster will come to your home. He has put his angels in charge of you to watch over you wherever you go. They will catch you in their hands so that you will not hit your foot on a rock. You will walk on lions and cobras; you will step on strong lions and snakes.

PSALM 91:9–13

MOGADISHU, SOMALIA, is probably not where you want to take a family vacation. At the time I'm writing this book, the US State Department's website warns: "Do not travel to Somalia due to crime, terrorism, civil unrest, health issues, kidnapping, and piracy."[1] Even so, my mom and I were headed there with author and speaker Bob Goff to do a food drop to people living in an area affected by famine, and to love on people. The woman sitting next to me on the plane asked us why we were going, then pleaded for us to turn around. "You need to go back home. It's too dangerous there," she said. Not exactly comforting words to hear.

We arrived to some chaos at the airport due to an active shooting. Our contact hurried us into a bulletproof car to whisk us to the hotel. In every direction we saw people draped with ammunition. The long list of questions just to check into our hotel room included documenting your blood type—and I didn't know mine. Can we say *intense*?

It's hard to sleep when you actually believe you're going to die. At full panic, I asked my mom to read Psalm 91 out loud. She opened her Bible and began to read, pausing to let the words sink in and calm me down: "Nothing bad will happen to you. . . . No disaster will come to your home. . . . He has put his angels in charge of you to watch over you wherever you go. . . ." (vv. 10–11). We declared God's Word over ourselves, believing that God had a plan for us to be there.

Accompanied by high security, over the next four days we surfed in the ocean with boys who had been trained as child soldiers and rescued from serving in terrorist groups. We held the babies of women who had been raped. We felt God's presence and experienced the beauty of His love—even in some of the darkest places.

My experience in Somalia reminds me of the story in Luke 8, where Jesus was in a boat with the disciples as they crossed a lake and He fell asleep. A strong wind came along and began blowing water into the boat. Even in the midst of that storm, Jesus was able to bring perfect peace to the situation. With just one command, He calmed the wind and the waves.

That's what Psalm 91 is to me—a reminder that God is always on alert and able to provide safety and protection, so I do not need to fear anything that may come my way.

If you are one of God's kids, then the same is true for you. The Lord is your protection. Your place of safety. A security guard once told me that the safest place you can be is in the center of God's will. Deep breath. Let's choose to live there, every day, in perfect peace even in the storm.

> **Father, I am overwhelmed by Your love for me and Your thoughtful care over every detail of my life. Thank You for understanding all of my fears—both real and imagined—and for giving me a way to connect with You through prayer. Even now I pray that in the midst of life's storms, You would cover me and my family as we step through this day. In Your Son's name I pray, amen.**

Find Your WAY

It's interesting how we seem to trust God more when we're in danger than in the ordinary challenges of life. Why? I think it's because typically, when you're in those frightening moments, you realize you're not God and that you are fully dependent on the One who is. Consider the difficulties you faced in the past week, even in the past month or two, and recall how God helped you through in spite of your fears for the worst. Then, slowly read aloud every word of Psalm 91. Write a note in the margin of your Bible with the date and a prayer for God's protection and provision, so that when He comes through (even in ways you might not expect!) you'll be able to note *that* date as well. It's the best way to remember, to document His goodness, and to personalize your Bible, making it your own God story.

THOSE WHO GO TO GOD MOST HIGH FOR SAFETY WILL BE PROTECTED BY THE ALMIGHTY. I WILL SAY TO THE LORD, "YOU ARE MY PLACE OF SAFETY AND PROTECTION. YOU ARE MY GOD AND I TRUST YOU."

Psalm 91:1–2

Wisdom DAY 32

DON'T TAKE AWAY THE HARD

It was good for me to be afflicted so that I might learn your decrees. The law from your mouth is more precious to me than thousands of pieces of silver and gold.

PSALM 119:71–72 NIV

WE WERE ON A FAMILY VACATION at the beach, and it was time for two-year-old Honey to go to sleep. The problem was she was in a new room, in a new bed, and she was scared. She kept calling out to me, asking me to come get her. I was just behind the door listening to her cry, so tempted to rush back in and forget nap time, but I didn't. I let her stay in that room for a little bit longer until she fell asleep, because I knew it was best for her. Sleep would give her strength and energy for the night of fun we had planned. But I also wanted to teach her to work through her fears when I knew she was perfectly safe and okay.

How often do you think God would rather rescue us from the things we struggle with than hear us cry out, wondering where He is? He is always a Good Father. He chooses the path that's best for us—not just what might make us happy in the moment.

Nature offers us so many examples that display this truth of struggle being good for us—the best thing for us—in the long run. A baby bird needs to fight to hatch from its shell so it grows strong enough to fly. Trees need wind resistance so that they grow their roots deep into the soil. Easy does not help us. We all need the struggle.

This is so opposite of what is trending right now in our culture, which is the pursuit of comfort. In fact, some people will likely be upset that I let Honey cry it out instead of going into her room to get her. If we're only concerned about creating comfort for our kids, we won't raise them to be strong people who can work through the hard things that life throws at them. The same is true for us. In our own desire for comfort, we miss out on the skills and strength we gain from working through challenges.

Think about that the next time you pray and the door doesn't open quickly, or when you show up but no one else does, or when Everything. Is. Just. Plain. Hard. You might want God to take away the hard, but what we learn from the struggle is worth more than thousands of pieces of gold and silver.

Find Your WAY

Christian and I want to help Honey grow stronger and more confident, even if she's not in a familiar place and even if it's dark. In the same way God allows things in our lives that'll strengthen us and prepare us for the future. Can you see where God is possibly wanting to help you grow? Maybe He's not saying, *I'm never opening the door for you,* but instead, *I am right here at the door with you. I am not going to leave you, but it's not yet time for that door to open.*

Father, I know You are good, but sometimes it's really tough to deal with hard people and situations and things— especially when they come one after the other. I trust You completely, but like Mark 9:24 says, *I do believe! Help me to believe more!* Deep breath. Thank You. Amen.

Wisdom DAY 33

ONE STEP AT A TIME

Your word is like a lamp for my feet and a light for my path.
I will do what I have promised and obey your fair laws.

PSALM 119:105–106

IF YOU'VE HEARD ME SPEAK, listened to my podcast, or read one of my books, then you probably know I like to be prepared for things. People often comment they're surprised I typically don't have any notes with me when I go up on stage. The fact is, I've prepared so much that I have all the notes memorized. Now, before you're impressed by that, I will say some of the heart behind that is a good thing, but another part of that is fear. I would always say that I wanted to let the Holy Spirit lead me. And while in some ways that's true, it was hard to let Him lead when I already had my whole talk planned out word for word, down to the minute.

One Tuesday night I was speaking to the campus ministry at Texas A&M when all of my normal preparation was suddenly met with an opportunity to lean into the Spirit's leading. For starters, I felt like the Lord was telling me to preach a different message than the one I'd prepared. That obviously left me with much less time to get ready than I would've liked. I did the best I could to plan and practice what I felt God was directing me to say, but when I got up to preach, right in the very middle of an analogy, I lost my train of thought. I stood there for a minute praying silently, asking God what He wanted to say to the people in front of me. And what began to come out of me was so much better than any sermon

I could have prepared—it truly was His Spirit leading the room.

The pastor noticed something had shifted. After the event he and his wife affirmed how powerful the moment had been—the one where they saw me allow God to truly lead. I was sharing things I had been talking to God about privately, thoughts only my journal had seen. And I realized something powerful—there is a difference in preparing your heart to live a godly life and trying to prepare for every minute of your life. One produces peace and the other produces fear and anxiety. Trusting the Holy Spirit requires faith. It also requires humility and openness.

> Father, I love Your Word and how it has withstood the test of time. It has been proven true over and over again! Thank You for speaking to me through it today and tomorrow, and the next day and the next. Remind me to meet with You within its pages. Your Word is truth and life and the heartbeat of my faith. I need it! I need You! I love You! Amen.

The next week the school pastors sent me a gift to encourage me to continue leaning into God's Spirit like I had done that night. The gift was a small oil lamp, like the ones in the Bible, and a letter quoting Psalm 119:105–106, our verses for today. The pastors told me, "The lamp in Psalms was just enough to light up one step at a time. You're not always going to see the whole path, but if you follow God's Word and His leading, He'll light your path one step at a time."

Life is challenging, often uncertain, and definitely messy. If you find yourself wandering around in the dark trying to find a path forward, then spend more time in God's Word. Here's another way to think about it. Every single night when we go to bed, Christian turns on the flashlight on his phone to walk from where he switches off the overhead light. It makes me giggle because it's the same path every single night, but I appreciate that he doesn't stumble and fall.

It's actually a good reminder that we can never get enough of God's Word—a lamp for our feet and a light for our path. Today, consciously, walk in humility as you let the Spirit and the Word of God lead you.

Find Your WAY

To become Bible-believing people we need to know not just the name of God— we need a relationship with Him and His Word. If you're having trouble understanding something you're reading, do some research and keep asking questions. I read from the *Enduring Word Bible Commentary*, and I also watch videos on BibleProject (Google it, it's awesome!). It's also helpful to talk with a pastor, mentor, or counselor. That will help illuminate the truth you might not otherwise have seen.

Wisdom DAY 34

A GIFT

*Children are a gift from the L*ORD*; babies are a reward. Children who are born to a young man are like arrows in the hand of a warrior. Happy is the man who has his bag full of arrows. They will not be defeated when they fight their enemies at the city gate.*

PSALM 127:3–5

IT'S SUCH A MIRACLE to carry a baby into the world. The Bible calls children a gift, a reward, and like arrows in the hand of a warrior. Now that we have two girls, Honey and Haven, I've recognized the depth of happiness that comes with the word *children*, which started for me when I first saw the plus sign on a pregnancy test. It was the absolute most exciting moment of my life! I jumped up and down with tears streaming down my face.

Although it's a huge blessing and a beautiful gift, bearing and raising children isn't easy. Talk to any mom of littles, and you'll hear how she often feels uncertain, overwhelmed, and just

Thank You, Father, for the miracle of life. On those days when it's hard, remind me that the gifts I've been given are just that—a gift, a blessing, and not a burden. No matter my situation, help me to keep my trust in You. Amen.

plain tired. I heard author and speaker Lisa Harper once say that before she adopted her daughter, she thought all of her mom friends around her were being dramatic! Some of you might feel that way too, if you're hearing your friends with kids complain about the lack of sleep, loads of laundry, temper tantrums, and all the messiness of motherhood. I will say, it's hard! But also, in the same breath, motherhood is the most incredible joy.

Moms, I think it is important to watch the way we talk about our children, and to make sure we are not complaining about the gift our children are. It is okay to be honest about the hard realities of parenting—because sometimes, it's really hard. But let's work to make sure our vulnerabilities help us and don't turn into simply complaining. And if you're really struggling with motherhood, by all means, please reach out to a trusted friend or therapist. I heard someone once say that it never makes anyone feel good to hear people complain about a gift God gave them. And that could go for anything! Don't take for granted the gifts God gave you. That may be your children, your talents, your job, your spouse, your family, your in-laws, or any blessing!

If you're in a season of feeling overwhelmed by a gift you've been given and that gift feels more like a burden, then stop and thank God for what He gave you. Then ask Him to help you navigate the challenges and savor the good of the gift.

Find Your WAY

God has a plan. Whether you're dealing with the struggles of having children or the struggles of not having children (or maybe you're not sure you *want* kids and you're navigating challenges around that), His plan is right and best for you for today. Tomorrow is another story. Your gift back to Him is how you live today. But if children are a part of your life, then recognize they're a gift. The most important thing is to be sure they have the light of Jesus shining in their life. Spend time today praying for your child. Pray that they will come to know Jesus as their personal Lord and Savior. Consider spending a few minutes each night reading through an age-appropriate devotional or Bible storybook. There are so many to choose from! Honey asks me almost every night to sing about Jesus as she raises her hands to worship. Then we pray. Find what works best for you. The main thing is to focus on Jesus.

Wisdom DAY 35

EAT THIS, NOT THAT

You made my whole being; you formed me in my mother's body. I praise you because you made me in an amazing and wonderful way. What you have done is wonderful. I know this very well. You saw my bones being formed as I took shape in my mother's body. When I was put together there, you saw my body as it was formed. All the days planned for me were written in your book before I was one day old.

PSALM 139:13–16

I HAD BECOME OBSESSED with getting healthy and fit. The unfortunate key word here is *obsessed*. Working to be healthy and fit is wonderful; being obsessed with it definitely is not.

To start, I thought I'd try a juice cleanse . . . but it didn't work out too well (I basically spent the week thinking about the virtues of a large pizza). I pushed myself pretty hard and ended up going too far, because what had started as a new focus on healthy eating and exercise became a very unhealthy mindset.

While there's nothing wrong with counting calories, making good food choices, or starting an exercise plan, constantly stressing out and dwelling on what we want to change about our bodies makes our minds super unhealthy. I've gone through seasons of letting a series of negative, even mean, thoughts invade me. If you let that kind of self-talk spin in your brain all the time, you'll be on the most unhealthy diet ever! It's essential to change our mindsets and fill ourselves with God's Word because self-confidence is about our hearts and minds as well as our bodies. (See 1 Corinthians 6:19–20 and 10:31.)

Positive self-talk is vitally important to our mental health *and* our physical health. I love what Dr. Daniel Amen, who has become a regular on my podcast, said about it: "I am not a fan of positive thinking . . . .I am a fan of accurate thinking." The great news is the Bible gives us truths to speak over ourselves. So if you can't find kind words to say, repeat the words from

> Lord, thank You for giving me the strength I need to overcome unhealthy thoughts that affect other areas of my life. Remind me of the truth, beauty, and confidence that come from knowing that You formed me and know me, and that I can fully trust You. I need You, I welcome You, I love You! Amen.

Psalm 139:13–16. The truth is, you actually need to believe you can change before anything happens. A negative obsession with your body isn't *good* for your body—or your soul.

I'm not in a place to advise you on your specific dietery and exercise needs. Each of us at some point or another may need to add more fruits and vegetables to our diet or eat less processed or sugary foods. We may need to exercise more. Or the opposite could be true—we may need to be eating more and exercising less. That is not what this is about.

Here's what I *can* say. When we find ourselves feeling stuck or struggling with body image, we need to remember that we were never intended to be exact replicas of one another, or someone we have seen. You were made to be *you*. And besides, being made in the image of God has a *much* deeper meaning than what you see in the mirror. You are so much more than what you look like! Look deeper. Think deeper. Your body is a temple, and I don't mean because of the way it looks, but what it hosts—the very presence of God!

I recently wrote a song called "Mirror" that's about my journey to having a healthy view of who God created me to be. The next time you're facing the question, "Should I eat this or eat that?" consider that the answer isn't as much about the food choice for your body as it is about what you're feeding your mind. Fuel your mind and your body with what you need so that you can do all that God has created you for!

Find Your WAY

What messages have you been telling yourself about how you look? Figure out where or who these messages are coming from. Then, think about if those messages hold what's best for you or what the current culture *thinks* is best for you. Your thoughts ultimately control you, so spend time thinking through where you want to be in five years, ten years, or even beyond that. Then ask God to help you work out a plan for your life that is both realistic and kind to yourself, knowing that all good things take time.

REFLECT on IT

As you reflect on the week, consider what you've learned about finding your way to the life God has mapped out for you. Highlight the statement(s) below that speak to you, then on the journaling lines write notes to yourself so you can remember God's truth and live it out every day.

- Defeat the plans of the Enemy by remembering that God is always on alert and able to provide safety and protection for whatever comes your way.

- What you learn as you struggle through hard times is worth more than actual silver and gold!

- To read the Bible and have a relationship with it is to be changed *by* it. God's Word is powerful!

- You have been given miraculous gifts. Treasure them. Ask God to help you navigate the hard and savor the good.

- We've each been made in amazing and wonderful ways, formed uniquely by God and original.

_____

_____

_____

REST and WORSHIP

God designed each week to include a day of rest. Use this day to take a time-out from the world and worship Him. Whether it's worship music that helps us turn our eyes and thoughts toward God, or a song that describes exactly how we're feeling, music is a gift that helps connect our spirit with God's Holy Spirit. Here are two of my favorites for this week:

- "Oceans," by Hillsong United, featuring Taya Smith

- "Trust in You," by Lauren Daigle

I have to admit, God, life is often hard and scary. Sometimes I find myself doubting that You see, You know, and You care. That's when I need to dig into Your Word that shines a light on my path. But I also trust in Your promise in Psalm 91, that You'll put Your angels in charge to watch over me wherever I go. Thank You for the gift of life—my own and the lives You have given me responsibility for. Once again, I dedicate myself to You. Amen.

8

Lord our Lord, your name is the most wonderful name in all the earth! It brings you praise in heaven above. You have taught children and babies to sing praises to you because of your enemies. And so you silence your enemies and destroy those who try to get even.

I look at your heavens, which you made with your fingers. I see the moon and stars, which you created. But why are people even important to you? Why do you take care of human beings? You made them a little lower than the angels and crowned them with glory and honor. You put them in charge of everything you made. You put all things under their control: all the sheep, the cattle, and the wild animals, the birds in the sky, the fish in the sea, and everything that lives under water.

Lord our Lord, your name is the most wonderful name in all the earth!

PSALM 8

Whoever loves money will never have enough money; whoever loves wealth will not be satisfied with it. This is also useless.

ECCLESIASTES 5:10

Wisdom DAY 36

LOOK UP!

> *Lord our Lord, your name is the most wonderful name in all the earth! It brings you praise in heaven above. You have taught children and babies to sing praises to you because of your enemies.*
>
> **PSALM 8:1–2**

GROWING UP, WHEN WE WERE DRIVING somewhere in my mom's car, we listened to all kinds of music. Except on Sundays. On that day we were only allowed to listen to Christian music, so I did because I had to. Then things changed as I got older. I now love worship music so much that it's truly all I want to listen to. I even started a worship band!

My first Christian music concert was MercyMe. I was probably seven or eight years old, and I went with my grandma. It was so worshipful that I think I cried the whole time. Why? Because when you participate in praising God it changes you. God's spirit comes, your spiritual eyes are opened wide, and you find your-self feeling elevated, as though you're in the heavens above, surrounded by angels who are praising God with you. It's a beautiful place, a holy place, and a safe place to reflect on your life—but with the perspective of heaven. At such a young age, I didn't have the language to describe why I felt like crying at that concert, but now I know—it was the Holy Spirit moving in me.

Praise music not only lifts our spirits, it helps us get our eyes off ourselves

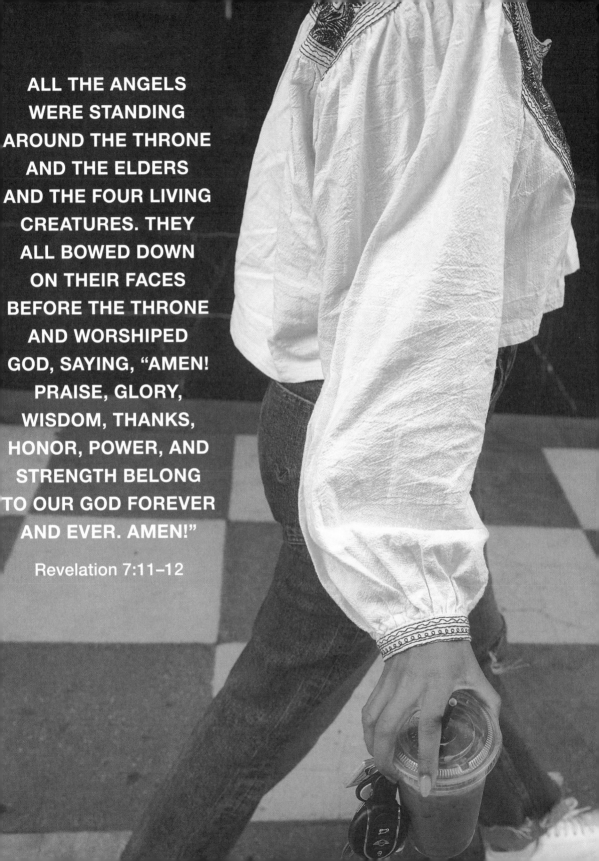

ALL THE ANGELS
WERE STANDING
AROUND THE THRONE
AND THE ELDERS
AND THE FOUR LIVING
CREATURES. THEY
ALL BOWED DOWN
ON THEIR FACES
BEFORE THE THRONE
AND WORSHIPED
GOD, SAYING, "AMEN!
PRAISE, GLORY,
WISDOM, THANKS,
HONOR, POWER, AND
STRENGTH BELONG
TO OUR GOD FOREVER
AND EVER. AMEN!"

Revelation 7:11–12

Find Your WAY

How do you feel about God? Find some paper and a pen, and handwrite a love letter to Him, thanking Him for who He is. If you have a favorite worship artist or a specific song that inspires you to draw close to God as your Father, bump it to your Favorites list and play it during your quiet time with Him. And don't forget to check out the songs listed at the end of each week. Hopefully you can find a new fave there.

Father, I worship You for who You are—holy, righteous, omnipotent, Creator, Redeemer, Almighty God, King of kings, and Lord of lords! Thank You for loving me and for providing everything I need. I dedicate my life to You. You alone I serve. Amen.

and sets our hearts and minds straight. When you're walking, you have to look up to see where you're going. In our spiritual life we need to do the same—to take a breath, look up, and remember where we are, where we're going, and Whose we are. It gives us the perspective we need to live a life worthy of the God who created us. And to consider that He isn't just a God who got things started and then backed off. He's involved in every aspect of our lives and the world around us.

When both Honey and Haven were in my womb, I would pray that God would establish strength in them as they praise Him. The inspiration for those prayers came from today's verse in Psalms. It's amazing to see that prayer play out in their lives! For instance, when Haven was just a couple months old, I could turn on a certain worship song, and it would immediately calm her crying.

Praise music is also a reminder of God's holiness, that He is pure, divine, and worthy of our praise. In fact, Psalm 22:3 tells us, "You sit as the Holy One. The praises of Israel are your throne." The word *throne* is a reference to a place to sit, to rest, to dwell—to inhabit. It's where we get the phrase "God inhabits the praise of His people."

It's in these special times of praise and worship that He draws nearer to us. What a beautiful, comforting thought! Join me, will you? Keep looking up!

Wisdom DAY 37

UP ALL NIGHT

And so you silence your enemies and destroy those who try to get even.

PSALM 8:2

WHILE PRAISING GOD CAN CHANGE our perspective, it's important to realize that the reason we have struggles in our lives is because we have an Enemy. Today's verse is a continuation of yesterday's that said, "You have taught children and babies to sing praises to you because of your enemies" (v. 2). *Your* enemies? Does this mean that God has enemies? Yes! And so do we. It's why we struggle, why we are fearful, and why we worry.

Have you watched the news lately? The world's headlines are sobering. There are wars, famine, terrorists, and devastating weather scenarios. Businesses are struggling, banks are failing, and people are angry. It's all out of control—*our* control.

Do we have an Enemy? Yes! First Peter 5:8 describes it this way: "Control yourselves and be careful! The devil, your enemy, goes around like a roaring lion looking for someone to eat." Okay, that's a visual I won't forget.

What are we to do? While we can't control the world around us, we *can* control ourselves, how we think, and what we allow into our surroundings.

On Day 35, I mentioned Dr. Daniel Amen, a good friend and author of several books who's helped me see there's a science to changing the pathways of your brain. It's both biblical and documented by scientific research that you can change the way

Dear Jesus, it's hard to navigate this life when it seems like so many things are stacked against me. Thank You for the reminder that when You walked among us, You had Your enemies as well. I know You truly understand. Help me to trust You and find gratefulness when it's hard to see reasons for either. I also pray that You'd help clear my mind of negative thoughts and give me a heart like Yours. Amen.

you think, and that doing so can change your habits (and ultimately your life). He said, "In three decades of working with patients, I've found that when you tell your brain what you want, your brain will help you make it happen."[1]

Author and speaker Joyce Meyer has a book called *Battlefield of the Mind* that is one of the most helpful books I have ever read on how to get control of your thought life. I suggest you read it if you're also having the same issues with control and worry.

Today's scripture says, "so you silence your enemies." The "you" here is God, but I believe it also includes us, with His help. When negative thoughts come into our minds, one way we can change the way we think is by determining that those thoughts will not be allowed to stay. Second Corinthians 10:4–5 says: "We fight with weapons that are different from those the world uses. Our weapons have power from God that can destroy the enemy's strong places. We destroy people's arguments and every proud thing that raises itself against the knowledge of God. We capture every thought and make it give up and obey Christ."

It's a powerful thing to realize that you can effect more change in your environment than the headlines can. This isn't the popular worldly message that you're powerful and can do whatever you want—it's the message that you have the power of God inside of you and therefore can effect the changes needed both inside of you and around you.

Don't ever forget that, with God, you have the power to silence the Enemy!

Find Your WAY

Worry can become a habit, just like anything else you become addicted to. What's important to note is that most of the things you worry about rarely come true. Researchers at Penn State University had participants write down their specific worries for ten days. Four times a day they were prompted by a text message to record any worries from the previous few hours. Every evening over the next thirty days, the participants reviewed their list of worries to see if any of them had come true. The result? Ninety-one percent of their worries were false alarms. And of the 9 percent that did come true, the outcome was better than expected in one-third of those.[2] Consider keeping your own worry log, and see how accurate it is. It might help you break a habit that absolutely brings more harm than good into your life.

Wisdom DAY 38

ONLY YOU CAN BE YOU

I look at your heavens, which you made with your fingers. I see the moon and stars, which you created. But why are people even important to you? Why do you take care of human beings? You made them a little lower than the angels and crowned them with glory and honor.

PSALM 8:3–5

ON JULY 20, 1969, astronauts Neil Armstrong and Buzz Aldrin made history by being the first men to walk on the moon. Just before those first steps outside of *Apollo 11*'s Eagle lunar module, with permission, Aldrin, an elder at Webster Presbyterian Church just outside of Houston, experienced the first-ever communion service on the moon.[1] Taking the bread and the wine, he read Psalm 8, declaring God's majesty and the incredible truth that the Creator of the earth, sun, moon, and stars also created us.[2] God topped us off with *glory*, which is defined by *Merriam-Webster* as "magnificence, splendor, and beauty,"[3] and He put us in charge. In the hierarchy of life, we are just under the angels but over everything else. Think about that for a minute.

Have you ever wondered to yourself, *Who am I?* One of my favorite characters in the Bible is Peter. Matthew 16 tells us that one day Peter and the other disciples were walking with Jesus when He asked them this same question, but in a different form. He said, "Who do people say the Son of Man is?" (v. 13).

Hold on—is it possible that Jesus cared what other people thought? Consider this: most likely Jesus was trying to get the disciples to verbalize who they thought He was for their own benefit, but also for them to consider who *they* were. The story concludes with a conversation between Jesus and Peter, when Jesus called Peter the rock that the church would be built on. (How's that for a life verse?!)

Here's the deal. We're all kind of like Peter—because when we recognize who Jesus is, He'll tell us who we are. Knowing that should directly impact what we choose to do. But there's also a noisy world continually telling us we are *this*, or not *that*, or

Thank You, Father, for creating me in Your image to be uniquely who I am. As I learn to let go of what the world thinks and become Your child, I pray You will fill me with Your thoughts, Your words, and Your will. I want to be wholly, completely, and uniquely Yours! Amen.

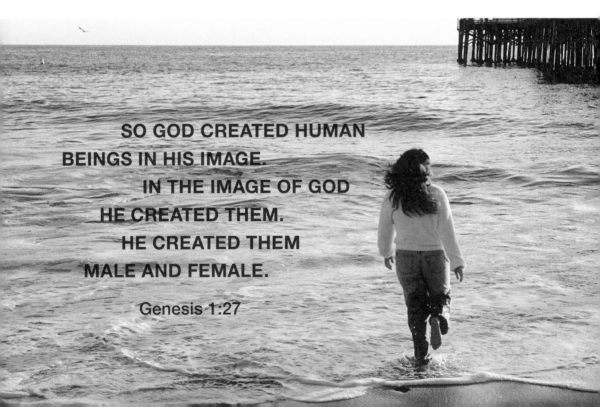

SO GOD CREATED HUMAN
BEINGS IN HIS IMAGE.
IN THE IMAGE OF GOD
HE CREATED THEM.
HE CREATED THEM
MALE AND FEMALE.

Genesis 1:27

Find Your WAY

Not long ago, while speaking to a group, I asked everyone to pull out their phones and look at themselves in their selfie cams. After an awkward amount of time, I asked them to describe what they saw. Then I preached a message about how God made them and why He made them. I asked them to consider a much deeper meaning and value for their life and then questioned if they saw themselves any differently. I wanted them from that point on, as they looked at their reflection, to not see the things they wanted to change but to see the reflection of God's light, life, and purpose in their eyes and on their face. Maybe today you need to do this. Describe yourself and then see how your perspective changes when you consider how God values you.

something completely different. We have personality tests like the Enneagram, Myers-Briggs, and others that give us insight, which is good to have. But honestly, if we're not careful, they can offer a list of excuses that we lean on, or they can take our focus away from who we are in Christ. So we can't stop there. We need to recognize, and even at times verbalize, that we are God's own—His loved and treasured creation, crowned in His glory and honor.

God created us in His image. It's why we'll only find our true identity in Him, but with our own unique DNA, fingerprints, abilities, weaknesses, and opportunities to serve Him. In the same way that only I can be—and should be—Sadie, only you can be you.

Let that sink in for a minute. *Only you can be you.* Only you can live out who you were originally created to be—one of the best gifts you could give the world! And if God made you in His image, and He did, then don't rob the world of seeing a side of God they've never seen before.

Wisdom DAY 39

THE POWER OF ALL CREATION

You put them in charge of everything you made. You put all things under their control: all the sheep, the cattle, and the wild animals, the birds in the sky, the fish in the sea, and everything that lives under water. LORD our Lord, your name is the most wonderful name in all the earth!

PSALM 8:6–9

SHE'S ALL OF SIX POUNDS, but she's got enough personality to be a whole person. Cabo, named to remind us of our honeymoon destination, is a Maltipoo with more ability to charm and less desire to obey than should be allowed. When we walk into the room, she makes her presence known with her excitement to see us. And though sometimes she's a lot of work, she totally completes our family of four. Well, five, when you count Cabo. And we do!

It's interesting to think that when God created the world, He put humans in charge of everything in it. Pretty crazy huh? Genesis 1:28 says, "Rule over the fish in the sea and over the birds in the sky and over every living thing that moves on the earth." Psalm 8 reminds us of this too.

Fish, birds, animals—and yes, even insects—add so much to our lives. It is actually crazy when you think about the gift these tiny bugs are, since they're part of the delicate balance of our ecosystem, which includes the air we breathe

> Thank You, Father, for the gift of animals that give us insights to life and nature beyond what we even realize. We know You have determined for them to be in our lives. May our care of them honor You and Your intentions. Amen.

Find Your WAY

Although I'm a dog owner, I've actually never been much of a pet person. On the other hand, my brother and sister-in-law are both obsessed with animals. Their love for them makes me want to love animals more. Consider the animals that are around you. Have you seen them through the lens of what God intended for us? For a period of time our family lived on land with horses. They brought us so much peace. Honey wanted to go see them every single day, and it became the sweetest thing ever. Don't miss the power of God's creation, which includes all of the uniquely beautiful creatures He created especially for us!

and the water we drink.[1] I studied the life of a plankton one time (I know, random), but I was blown away by all of the purpose God's put inside of these microscopic organisms that float in water. Without them we pretty much wouldn't be breathing because plankton produce 50 to 80 percent of the world's oxygen.[2] And then, there are the animals that get to be our friends like Cabo Pop (that's our nickname for her!).

Even if you don't have your own dog or cat, or horse or chicken, or even a good ol' betta fish, you likely know someone who does. So spend time with that amazing animal, just to see another form of how awesome God's creation is. Believe it or not, there are even scientific health benefits to being around animals. Plus I've heard stories of people meeting their spouse when they came to meet their dog! You never know what pet owner out there may become your new best friend—just saying.

Wisdom DAY 40

OOOH, I WANT ONE!

Whoever loves money will never have enough money; whoever loves
wealth will not be satisfied with it. This is also useless.

ECCLESIASTES 5:10

ONE TIME I WAS READING A BOOK that got into the topic of materialism and all the things we spend our money on. It was bringing up questions like, "Do we have money or does it have us?" And, "Are we being good stewards of what we've acquired?" Then to top it off, the author referenced Matthew 6:21: "Your heart will be where your treasure is."

This all made perfect sense to me . . . except in that moment, I'd just made a somewhat significant purchase, and I wasn't sure if I was feeling convicted or guilty. (Moms, I am sure you can relate. Sometime it can feel weird to buy something for yourself when you have everyone else to buy for.) And then I read that the point was not to feel guilty about the last thing we'd bought. It's okay to take a vacation, it's okay to buy something nice. But at the end of the day, we need to consider that God is looking at our stewardship. And if He can trust us with the little things, He knows He can trust us with the bigger ones (Luke 16:10).

I almost never buy myself jewelry, but on a family vacation a necklace caught my eye while I was browsing in a shop. I knew instantly that I wanted it. When

I went to pay for it, I realized it wasn't just a casual piece of jewelry—it was the real thing. I told the clerk to put it back, that I was sorry, it was a mistake.

But I was in trouble. I'd already put it on and loved it even more than when I'd first seen it.

Later that night I was talking to Christian. "That necklace was so pretty! Why did I try it on? It's the kind I could wear every day. I could even change the pendant. Then maybe like in five years, you could find a new pendant for it, and that could be like our thing."

Can you say *rationalization*?

The next day came and went, and that night I brought it up again to Christian: "So, I was thinking about that necklace, and . . ."

He gently stopped me. "I have never seen you care about anything materialistic like this in our whole relationship. You keep bringing it up. You clearly want it—you should just go get it."

"No," I said, "I can't buy that for myself. This is just ridiculous, it's not even that special . . . I don't know why, I just like it so much."

The next day I received a work request I wasn't anticipating. Christian said, "If you do that work, then I think you should buy the necklace. It's perfect timing. You should do this for yourself. Besides, it's not like we aren't stewarding our money well."

> Lord, please keep me mindful of the ways I worship things more than You. Help me to loosen my grip on them so that I can in turn grasp on to more of You. Amen.

I am not saying that every time you buy something you need to also do something spiritual alongside. However, the amount of the necklace was the same amount I had planned on giving this charity that I had not gotten around to. You might be thinking that I was overthinking this entire situation, but honestly, I'm glad I felt the hesitation that I did. It's always smart to manage your money, but it's especially important for us now as a young couple—we've got a house and two kids and many things in front of us. It is also smart to consider why you want something in the first place: is this something you're going to toss aside in

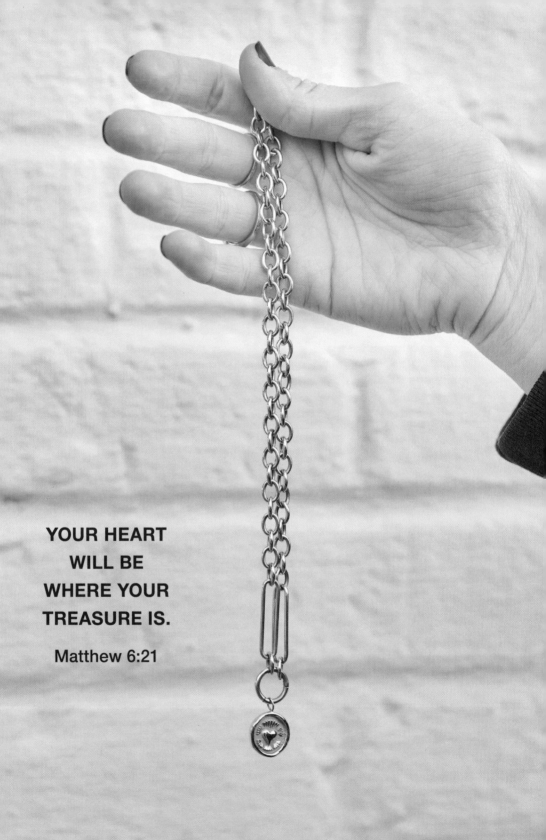

YOUR HEART WILL BE WHERE YOUR TREASURE IS.

Matthew 6:21

a few weeks, or something you'll treasure for a while?

I thought about it for a long time, and eventually I decided to buy the necklace. In the process I acknowledged that the necklace was temporary, like everything else we posess on earth. And because the pendant is a heart, I determined to use it to remind me of Matthew 6:21 so that I wouldn't forget that my heart would follow anything I treasured.

Listen, I think what's most important when it comes to making a purchase is that your priorities are straight and your heart is pure. And I'm definitely not telling you to stay away from fun. Girl, go buy that necklace if you want to! But remember, we carry nothing from this earth into eternity with us. Even our physical bodies go back to the earth. It's totally okay to spend the money we've earned on ourselves now and then, but it's also important to remember the real treasure is the one thing that will never rust, unravel, or fade away—our life with God through His Son, Jesus.

Find Your WAY

Where are your treasures? Consider this scenario: Your house is on fire, and you have five minutes to run in and get whatever you want (trust me, that necklace isn't anywhere *close* to the list of things I am grabbing). What will you take out with you? Pull out your Notes app, and list a few things. Then look at the list and reflect on why each item is so meaningful.

REFLECT on IT

As you reflect on the week, consider what you've learned about finding your way to the life God has mapped out for you. Highlight the statement(s) below that speak to you, then on the journaling lines write notes to yourself so you can remember God's truth and live it out every day.

- Worship puts life into perspective. It strengthens us, encourages us, and reminds us of God's holiness.

- You have the power to silence the Enemy.

- God created us in His own image, which is why we will only find our identity in Him.

- Animals add so much to our lives. Don't forget to see them as the gift they are, even if you, like me, are not much of an animal person.

- Don't concentrate on treasures for yourself on earth. Instead focus on the real treasure—the life of Christ in you!

_____

_____

_____

REST and WORSHIP

God designed each week to include a day of rest. Use this day to take a time-out from the world and worship Him. Whether it's worship music that helps us turn our eyes and thoughts toward God, or a song that describes exactly how we're feeling, music is a gift that helps connect our spirit with God's Holy Spirit. Here are two of my favorites for this week:

- "Give Us Clean Hands," by Chris Tomlin

- "I'll Give Thanks," by Housefires, featuring Kirby Kaple

Thank You, Jesus, for the things You give us to enjoy while we're here on earth, but keep us ever mindful that our true identity is not in things but in You alone. We worship and praise Your holy name! Amen.

Those who work hard make a profit, but those who only talk will be poor.

PROVERBS 14:23

It takes wisdom to have a good family, and it takes understanding to make it strong. It takes knowledge to fill a home with rare and beautiful treasures.

PROVERBS 24:3–4

He brought me to the banquet room, and his banner over me is love.

SONG OF SONGS 2:4

Catch the foxes for us—the little foxes that ruin the vineyards while they are in blossom.

SONG OF SONGS 2:15

I woke you under the apple tree where you were born; there your mother gave birth to you. Put me like a seal on your heart, like a seal on your arm. Love is as strong as death; jealousy is as strong as the grave. Love bursts into flames and burns like a hot fire. Even much water cannot put out the flame of love; floods cannot drown love. If a man offered everything in his house for love, people would totally reject it.

SONG OF SONGS 8:5–7

Wisdom DAY 41

WORK IS WORK

Those who work hard make a profit, but those who only talk will be poor.

PROVERBS 14:23

IF WE TOOK A POLL ASKING, "Do you want to be successful in everything you do?" I think we'd get a 100 percent response of "Absolutely, yes!" But if the next question were, "How hard are you willing to work for it?" the truth would show answers from one end of the spectrum to the other.

Why is work so hard sometimes?

To answer that we'll need to go back to the beginning of time and look at the very first couple. You can read the full story in Genesis, where in chapter two God ordains work as a good thing, and then in chapter three, we are introduced to a visitor: "Now the snake was the most clever of all the wild animals the LORD God had made" (v. 1). You know the rest of the story—how lies were told, decisions were made, and actions sealed all of our fates: "So I will put a curse on the ground, and you will have to work very hard for your food" (Genesis 3:17).

Praise God that doesn't have to be the end of the story! Though God's original intention for us was corrupted, the sacrifice of Christ on the cross offers a way for every area of our lives to be redeemed. How? On Day 26, we read Colossians 3:23: "In all the work you are doing, work the best you can. Work as if you were doing it for the Lord, not for people." Pastor Matt Chandler once told me he loves thinking that every day he gets to go to work *with* and *for* His dad, meaning God the Father. We all have the same incredible opportunity! So with heart and soul do your job well, whatever it may be, like you're doing it with and for the Lord.

The truth is that we were created to work. We were made for it. Work brings so many good things to our lives, benefits that go beyond income. For example, it . . .

- builds our identity, self-esteem, and stability
- motivates us to establish goals and become more organized
- provides ways to interact with others, offering us a sense of belonging
- puts structure in our day

The truth is, only a life lived for God has purpose and meaning. You can live for God in any job you have, but doing it without Him in the equation? That's when we become like hamsters stuck in the vicious wheel that spins around and around but leads us nowhere—except into a permanent state of exhaustion, anxiety, and dissatisfaction.

It's also essential that we have an attitude of gratitude, being thankful and content with where we are, along with a willingness to do the job until God directs us somewhere else. If by chance you find yourself caught in that transition, or if you're in a starter or temporary job, recognize that and see what God has for you to learn right now. Good work builds upon good work! Then do the *really* hard work of waiting for Him to show you the way. I promise He will!

Father, I know that You designed the world with a plan that requires us to be involved and to work. Thank You for the many benefits that come with this design. But I need Your help when things get out of whack. And if You have something different for me, help me to trust that You'll lead me to the next place in Your time and in Your way. My heart's desire is to live and work for You. Amen.

GOD HAS MADE US WHAT WE ARE. IN CHRIST JESUS, GOD MADE US TO DO GO[OD] WORKS, WHICH GOD PLANNED IN ADVAN[CE] FOR US TO LIVE OUR LIVES DOING.

Ephesians 2:10

Find Your WAY

Create a timeline of your places of employment and positions you've held since your first job. Include any activity that required you to show up and be responsible for something, even if you weren't actually paid for it. Don't worry if you have just one or two things listed—spend a little extra time thinking about where you might have gone and why you didn't. Then dream about where you want to go. This can be as simple or as complicated as you'd like for it to be. The point is to think about what you've done, what you'd like to do, and why.

Wisdom DAY 42

LOVING YOUR SPACE

It takes wisdom to have a good family, and it takes understanding to make it strong. It takes knowledge to fill a home with rare and beautiful treasures.

PROVERBS 24:3–4

I CAME ACROSS A PIECE OF COOL abstract art that had the funniest name. The artist had titled it *The Urgency of Toast with Honey.* I liked that name because it was different and unexpected. I appreciated the creativity to even think of something like that! I was thinking I could hang it in the entryway of our house, but my sister Bella, an art student, saw the piece and said, "It just feels stressful to me." After I gave it another look, I realized it *was* a little stressful. It was intended to symbolize something urgent and pressing. Like, "Hurry! The honey is about to drip off the toast!" While I still like the piece, I decided it's not the first message I want to give to people walking into our house, including us.

The space we live in, whether a room, an apartment, or a house, often reflects where we are in life. For instance, when I'm really stressed and have a lot going on, I have piles stacked up all over my house (which makes me *more* stressed). Then, when I come out of the stressful time, I see those piles in a different way and begin cleaning them up.

Sometimes, I think we get so busy, we don't stop to be intentional about our homes and our environments. For example, Christian and I stayed in the guest house on my parents' property for three years after we were married. It was built by the previous owner in an entirely different style than what we would've chosen. With dark walls and drippy candlelight fixtures, it not only wasn't my style, it was also kind of depressing! It wasn't until we painted the house all white and changed some of the lighting that we began to feel at home.

No doubt our environment affects us. But we often have more control over it than we realize. We can love our spaces and help ourselves by removing the clutter, repainting the walls, and choosing happier art. Or simply by doing the dishes and cleaning up the mess! Even the smallest things—a plant, a candle, some favorite photos—can add something that will make your home more *you*.

In our verse for today God reminds us that we need wisdom, understanding, and knowledge to have a beautiful home that sets the stage for how we live our lives. But we also need God's presence because, unless we make Him a part of our home, it won't matter if we have the latest art or architecture. We won't find peace unless we invite Him into our space. He is the One who brings love and blessings. From there the doors are open to all kinds of possibilities, leaving us free to dream and think and plan and grow, knowing God is right there with us.

Father, thank You for giving me a place to live. Please make Your love, kindness, and presence felt to anyone who walks in the door. Protect us from the Evil One. We dedicate this space to You. Amen.

Find Your WAY

Dedicating our homes to God makes them more peaceful and comfortable, which influences those who live there or who walks in the door. To that end, here are a few ideas to consider:

- Clean out anything that isn't God-honoring, including books, movies, art, posters, and video games. I'm not saying everything needs to be faith-filled or explicitly Christian, but consider what you allow in—because a home filled with God's presence brings peace.
- Gather a few Christian friends and family to participate in a prayer of blessing with you when you move to a new home.
- Walk through your home and pray in each room. Dedicate each space to God, thanking Him for His provision and asking for His protection and blessing on your home and everyone in it.
- Turn on worship music and let it play as background noise in your home. It's amazing how much peace it will add to the atmosphere.
- In the Bible, fire often represents God's presence. Light a candle as a representation of God's presence in your home.

Wisdom DAY 43

LOVE, GOD

He brought me to the banquet room, and his banner over me is love.

SONG OF SONGS 2:4

POETRY, ONE OF THE MOST BEAUTIFUL forms of writing, often rises from an overflow of powerful feelings, which could be why poems can provoke intense emotions like joy, sorrow, anger, and love. My little sister Bella writes poetry. It always amazes me to hear her words arranged in such a beautiful way. When she is able to express herself with this extra depth of emotion, it helps me better relate to what she's gone through in her life.

We see that emotion in the Song of Songs, which literally means "the greatest song," and is a collection of ancient Israelite love poetry thought to have been written by King Solomon. It's a collection of words and metaphors that speak to the joy of physical attraction and the intense desire of a man and a woman who fall in love, become engaged, marry, and live their lives together.

One of the bedrocks of society is marriage between a man and a woman. Song of Songs illustrates this essential relationship with garden imagery that recalls the first couple God created. It also reminds us that His intention for Adam and Eve was to feel unified and safe and to have a relationship untainted by sin.[1] Honestly, I spent most of my life skipping over this book in the Bible because I had heard it was intense. And, well, it is! Before Christian and I got married, we read *The Mingling of Souls* by Matt Chandler, which explains Song

Father, I am overwhelmed with the thought that You love me. *Me!* Not what I do but who I am, Your beloved creation born with intention and purpose. Thank You, Jesus, for Your gift of salvation — Your display of ultimate love and sacrifice. Amen.

of Songs as the most beautiful picture of love between a man and a woman. And it helped me get rid of any fears I had going into our wedding night.

It might be surprising to you that relationships, sex, and intimacy were all God's ideas that He intended for us as a gift to enjoy. Unfortunately, sex in our culture has become almost exclusively a physical thing, which is probably why I had a lot of anxiety around it. Matt said, "God's plan is for a man and a woman in the bond of the marriage covenant to have their souls—not just their bodies—become one."[2] This divine perspective on human love in the Song of Songs is a breath of fresh air in our times of confusion regarding love and sexuality.

Another widely accepted interpretation of the Song of Songs is that it points to Christ's love, His literal delight for His bride, the church. And the grace He offers in laying down His life for us—the ultimate act of love.[3]

Do you realize how very much God loves you? It's so much more than we can comprehend! More than a spouse who adores you. More than a parent who is thrilled to have you. God loves you even *more*. Let's slow down long enough to dwell on this, and even picture Jesus bringing us into a large banquet room with a sign over our heads that says, "I absolutely adore this person!" Let that sink in as you go about your day today. You are loved!

Find Your WAY

It's not abiding by rules or fear that brings us to the Kingdom; it's the love of God that transforms us. Once you begin to recognize the depth and breadth of that love, consider how you're supposed to treat others—especially the person you're married to. Consider how it might be water for a dying-of-thirst world that doesn't realize that kind of unconditional love exists—not just in marital relationships, but in how you treat your neighbor, your coworker, even that someone you might consider to be your enemy.

Wisdom DAY 44

DON'T TRIP!

Catch the foxes for us—the little foxes that ruin the
vineyards while they are in blossom.

SONG OF SONGS 2:15

OUR SONG OF SONGS VERSE for today reminds us that "little foxes" are destructive and can cause a lot of damage. Scholars say that in this setting, foxes are synonymous with the sinful desires and passions that rise up in us and can include things such as our thoughts, words, and actions. No matter how small or insignificant these "creatures" might seem, they can eventually be caught so that they don't ruin the blossoming vineyard—the romantic relationship.[1]

Today, let's focus on one little fox—harsh words, spoken without thought. Whether they come from a simple misunderstanding or emotions rooted in superiority, selfishness, jealousy, or even unforgiveness, harsh words have the power to put a wedge in a relationship. We've all been there, saying something we feel strongly about in the moment, but later we realize our words were petty or mean. Once they're out there, though, you can't reel those words back in. And unless you deal with them as quickly as possible, they'll continue to inflict pain and cause ruin.

There have been times when I've been jealous of someone. When I let that jealousy live in my head and later spoke of that person, I realized the way I was talking about them was negative—which was so unfair to them. All because I let a sprig of jealousy take root and grow in my mind.

Little things can also work for good in your life. The Song of Songs is dripping with words of love and adoration worthy of a greeting card line. They remind us that compliments are important and should be the norm in any love relationship. So consider implementing the practice of giving your spouse (or someone else you love) at least one compliment a day. This is easier for some than for others, but if you're sincere, it's a way to truly honor your spouse.

A compliment can be sweet, but it should also be honest, which intensifies its power. My great-grandma once gave me a compliment. I replied, "That's sweet!" In return she said, "I'm not being sweet, I'm being honest!" which sent the words even deeper into my soul!

The same is true in our relationship with God. As we remind ourselves of His wonderful goodness and mercy, those words of praise and gratefulness to Him will come back to lift us up.

The moral of this story? Be on the lookout for the little foxes in your life—stumbling blocks that often begin with negative thoughts but quickly become words and actions that trip us up. Instead, use kind, thoughtful, complimentary words that will become stepping stones to the strongest forever relationship of all.

Father, You have given us the Bible, Your Word, to help us in every area of our lives. Thank You for this reminder from Song of Songs, that we are to be mindful of the little foxes that come in to ruin our relationships. Help me "catch" and stop them. Then fill me with Your Spirit so that I can have Your wisdom to use words that build up instead of tear down. Amen.

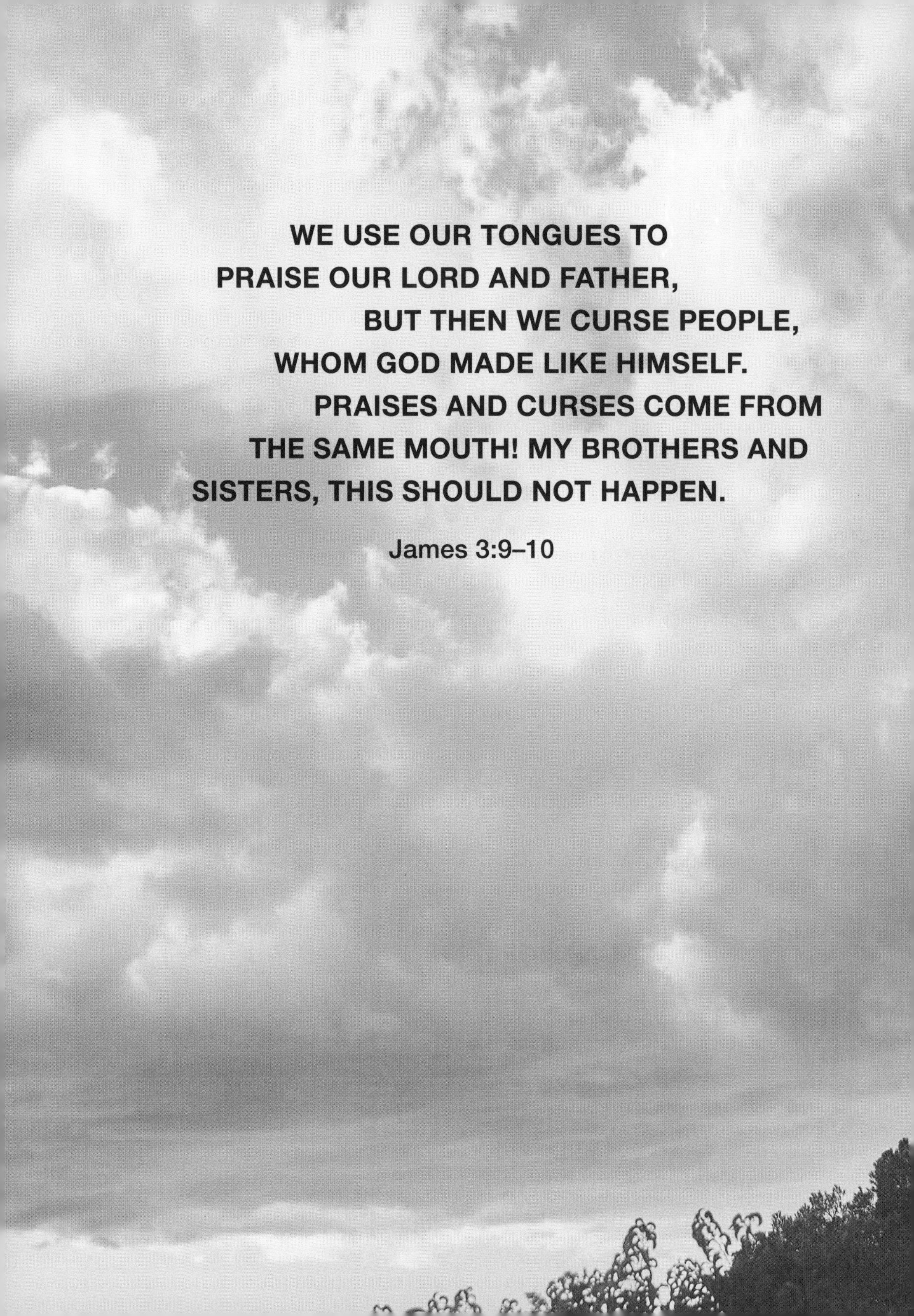

WE USE OUR TONGUES TO
PRAISE OUR LORD AND FATHER,
BUT THEN WE CURSE PEOPLE,
WHOM GOD MADE LIKE HIMSELF.
PRAISES AND CURSES COME FROM
THE SAME MOUTH! MY BROTHERS AND
SISTERS, THIS SHOULD NOT HAPPEN.

James 3:9–10

Find Your WAY

The book of James has almost an entire chapter on the power of the tongue and our attempts to control the things we say. In fact, James says the tongue is "like a fire" or a wild animal that can't be tamed (James 3:6–8). That's a lot of power! Read through James 3, underline the verses that speak to you, and note the power that your words have.

Wisdom DAY 45

THE POWER AND PURPOSE OF RELATIONSHIPS

I woke you under the apple tree where you were born; there your mother gave birth to you. Put me like a seal on your heart, like a seal on your arm. Love is as strong as death; jealousy is as strong as the grave. Love bursts into flames and burns like a hot fire. Even much water cannot put out the flame of love; floods cannot drown love. If a man offered everything in his house for love, people would totally reject it.

SONG OF SONGS 8:5–7

WHEN I WAS A KID, I went through a season when every time I ate an apple I'd take the seeds out to the yard, bury them, and water them. But I never marked where the seeds were so that I could continue to water and nurture them. The result? We had seeds planted all over our yard but no apple trees. It's the same with our relationships. Whether romantic, family, besties, or a new friend, these essential human connections need continued nurturing and the time and space to grow.

The Song of Songs' story of a passionate, romantic relationship concludes with a reminder that love is poweful and intense—it can be beautiful and life-giving or dangerous and destructive. That's why it's so important to pay attention to and properly cultivate our relationships.

———

"If you leave, we're breaking up."

My eighteen-year-old father Willie spoke these words to my seventeen-year-old mother Korie, whom he'd been dating, when she told him that she had decided to leave Louisiana and attend Harding University in Arkansas. They had met in third grade. My mom actually wrote in her third-grade journal how cute he was! (Yes, they are those people.) But that night, right before college, it felt like their relationship was over.

My mom stuck to her decision, and soon she was off to school and a roommate she didn't know.

Two weeks into that first semester, my dad called her to say, "I think I've had a change of heart." While their time of separation had been excruciatingly hard, it was also an important time for both of them to think, pray, and consider how they needed to restructure and cultivate their relationship. They did, of course, get back together and later got married. They learned that love is strong but, like a seed that has been planted, it needs tending along with time and space to grow.

> Thank You, Jesus, for the gift of love, the blessing of relationships, and how they help to cultivate Your character in me. Give me wisdom in what I say and do so that I can care for others in a way that helps them grow and honors You. Amen.

As you plant new seeds of connection with others, it's not only important to remember where you planted them, but you also need to continue to tend them with the time, love, and care they deserve. (Just think—if my mom and dad hadn't tended the seeds they planted, I wouldn't be here!) Love is powerful, friend. Let's make sure we're tending to our relationships in ways that are harnessing that power for life-giving good.

God doesn't just symbolize love; He *is* love. And He made us for relationship—with Him and with one another.

MOST IMPORTANTLY, LOVE
EACH OTHER DEEPLY,
BECAUSE LOVE WILL CAUSE
PEOPLE TO FORGIVE EACH
OTHER FOR MANY SINS.

1 Peter 4:8

Find Your WAY

Think about your relationships. Is the time you're spending with others a time of nurturing and growth, or is it more dangerous and destructive? If the situation is out of balance, then it might be time to rethink the connection. Don't forget to pray and trust God's leading.[1]

REFLECT on IT

As you reflect on this week, consider what you've learned about finding your way to the life God has mapped out for you. Highlight the statement(s) below that speak to you, then on the journaling lines write notes to yourself so you can remember God's truth and live it out every day.

- Work brings good things to our lives, but only a life lived for God has purpose or meaning.

- Find love, peace, and blessing in your home by inviting God to come into it.

- God loves us more than we could ever comprehend or imagine.

- Use your words as stepping stones to build good, strong relationships—not as stumbling blocks that cause harm and division.

- God made us for relationship—with Him and with one another.

_____

_____

_____

REST and WORSHIP

God designed each week to include a day of rest. Use this day to take a time-out from the world and worship Him. Whether it's worship music that helps us turn our eyes and thoughts toward God, or a song that describes exactly how we're feeling, music is a gift that helps connect our spirit with God's Holy Spirit. Here are two of my favorites for this week:

- "Way Maker," by Leeland

- "Just Want You," by The Belonging Co, featuring Sarah Reeves

Lord Jesus, I love how Your plan always includes what's best for me. Thank You for Your constant love and for providing the wisdom I need to live my life in honor of You. Amen.

10

The LORD is my shepherd; I have everything I need. He lets me rest in green pastures. He leads me to calm water. He gives me new strength. He leads me on paths that are right for the good of his name. Even if I walk through a very dark valley, I will not be afraid, because you are with me. Your rod and your shepherd's staff comfort me. You prepare a meal for me in front of my enemies. You pour oil of blessing on my head; you fill my cup to overflowing. Surely your goodness and love will be with me all my life, and I will live in the house of the LORD forever.

PSALM 23

Wisdom DAY 46

MY SHEPHERD

The LORD is my shepherd; I have everything I need.

PSALM 23:1

THROUGHOUT THE BIBLE, Christians are referred to as sheep. Have you ever wondered why? At an IF:Gathering, author Ann Voskamp once interviewed a shepherd as she held a lamb. We learned how important the relationship is between sheep and the shepherd who is always providing for them and protecting them. That's so sweet! But also it's widely accepted that sheep . . .

- get super anxious but calm down when they recognize the shepherd's voice
- aren't supposed to carry a heavy load
- follow others without a second thought
- lack discernment—they'll settle for drinking a dirty puddle in front of them instead of going to a clean stream ten feet away.[1]

While the analogy is true, it's not all that flattering. So let's think about it this way. In Jesus' day, sheep were treated as prized possessions. They provided meat, milk, and wool and also produced offspring. But because of their many vulnerabilities, they needed someone to take care of them, someone they could trust. A shepherd was that person, the one who brought them comfort and strength, who made sacrifices to protect them, and who led them to the good pasture so that they could stay healthy.

Psalm 23, one of the most well-known and beloved passages in the Bible, was written by King David, a former shepherd. He knew all about sheep and had no problem making the analogy to how God watches over us.

The second part of today's verse, "I have everything I need," reminds us of God's specific promise to provide for us. Some Bible versions say "I shall not want"; others say "I lack nothing" or "I don't need a thing." Whichever translation you read, the point is clear—God takes really good care of us, no matter what situation we may find ourselves in or how sheep-like we might behave![2] Consider this: David was often in danger and in trouble—facing Goliath, running from Saul who was trying to kill him, sometimes even needing food and water. Through it all God provided for him and protected him. And ultimately, David lived a life far greater than his wildest dreams.

> Father in heaven, thank You for being my personal Shepherd and for caring for me in ways I'll likely never even know. I recognize that with You I am safe and loved, and that I have everything I need. I am listening for Your voice. Guide me in Your perfect ways. Amen.

God does the same for us today. Along with those close to me, I have personally experienced the Lord providing exactly *what* I needed *when* I needed it. Whatever happens, whatever we might need, God is there to watch over us and care for us. Notice that I'm not saying God will always give you what you want, but I do believe He will provide everything you need.

He is the Good Shepherd, and we are His treasured little lambs.

Find Your WAY

In his book *Traveling Light*, author Max Lucado recalled the story of a chaplain in the French army who used Psalm 23 to encourage soldiers before battle. The chaplain would have the soldiers hold up one hand, extend their fingers and, beginning with the little finger, count toward the thumb while quoting the words "The Lord is my shepherd." When they got to "my," which was the index finger, he told them to grab on to it and hold it, helping them recognize that God indeed was their—and our—personal Shepherd.[3] Try it yourself. And while you're holding on, thank God for His heart and His promises.

Wisdom DAY 47

MINUTE-LONG VACATIONS

He lets me rest in green pastures. He leads me to calm water. He gives me new strength. He leads me on paths that are right for the good of his name.

PSALM 23:2–3

EVERY DAY ON MY DRIVE home from work, during my first year of motherhood, I would pass a house with two elderly people sitting together in their rocking chairs on the front porch. Seeing them always made me smile as I'd think to myself, *One day I'm going to write them a letter and tell them how much seeing them together gives me hope for what I want my marriage to look like in the future.*

But one day they weren't there. I didn't see them the next day, or the next. Day after day they didn't appear on the front porch. Eventually, I saw a sign in their yard advertising an estate sale, and my heart sank. I didn't know if they had passed away or what might have happened—but I'd never written that letter. Noting the details of the estate sale, I made it a priority to show up for it.

In the days leading up to the sale, I asked the Lord what I should do. I ended up withdrawing some cash to take to the sale and drove over. I looked for the couple, but they weren't there. Instead, there was another woman running the sale. I asked her about the previous owners, and she said they were her parents and had recently passed away within one month of each other. She smiled as she described the people they'd been and the love they'd shared.

I explained why I was there and the impact the couple had had on me from afar, simply by seeing them each evening sitting in their rocking chairs, enjoying each other's company. I expressed how sad I was that I never wrote them a letter thanking them for their example. Then I gave her the cash, hoping to bless her. With tears in her eyes, she hugged me.

As I looked around the estate sale, hoping to find something that reminded me of that sweet couple, I saw a small wooden plaque with a poem on it called "Slow Me Down, Lord." I knew I was taking this home, because if I had just slowed down long enough to write that letter, I would've had the opportunity to meet this couple. The poem is several verses long and includes these lines:

> Teach me the art of taking minute vacations,
> of slowing down to look at a flower,
> to chat with a friend,
> to pat a dog,
> to read a few lines from a good book.[1]

No doubt you've had days when all you wanted to do was retreat. Maybe you feel that way right now! You dream of a day when there's no to-do list,

COME TO ME, ALL OF
YOU WHO ARE TIRED
AND HAVE HEAVY LOADS,
AND I WILL GIVE YOU REST.

Matthew 11:28

no demands, no pressure. As you close your eyes and breathe deeply, you might imagine sitting in a cozy cabin overlooking the mountains, or lying on a tropical beach with no cell service. Getting away might not be an option right now. But even though the Bahamas is out of reach today, you can still take a little vacation to regain some calm.

It's so natural for our schedules to get jam-packed, to feel like we have no time to stop or to rest. But finding quiet, peace, renewed strength, and hope is like a mini-vacation for your soul. These two verses in Psalm 23 offer the promise of restoration, along with strength for the journey and the hope that things will be okay.

We might just need to slow our pace. Maybe we put the phone down, play with the kids, read a book, go on a walk, play cards, dance, draw, hang out with friends, or simply sit with Jesus. These are what green pastures and calm waters look like to me. They bring me into His presence and give me strength.

Find Your WAY

Think through what restores your soul. Is it going for a long walk? Working out at the gym? Playing tennis? Gardening? Drawing? Reading? Recognize whatever hobby or activity you enjoy, and then intentionally add it to your calendar. You may find these green pastures and calm water bring you strength for entering into the paths that are right for the good of His name.

Father, I am so grateful for Your provision in all things, including rest when I'm weary and restoration when I'm wrecked. I give my life in service to You. Amen.

Wisdom DAY 48

NEVER WALK ALONE

Even if I walk through a very dark valley, I will not be afraid, because you are with me. Your rod and your shepherd's staff comfort me.

PSALM 23:4

SO, PICTURE THIS. You're walking in darkness, unable to see where to safely place your foot for the next step, and the next. And you're in a valley, which makes you feel even more isolated. Besides a bright light, what else would make a difference?

Not being alone.

Because having someone beside you changes *everything*.

After I moved from Nashville back to Louisiana, I had many friends come to visit me. One night I wanted to take them somewhere special, and I wanted to walk there. It was 10:00 p.m. when we decided to walk the half mile to the location. No one hesitated—we simply walked out the door and headed in the right direction. About halfway through the journey, we started to laugh, admitting we *never* would have done this alone, but something about us all being together made the situation seem not scary at all.

So many of the psalms of King David, who had been a shepherd boy, describe him as being surrounded by enemies planning to attack him. Fear is immobilizing, so David determined to put his thoughts and trust in God. Psalm

56:3–4 says it this way: "When I am afraid, I put my trust in you. In God, whose word I praise—in God I trust and am not afraid. What can mere mortals do to me?" (NIV). Everything changes when the Good Shepherd comes in to be *with* us and to walk alongside us.

Verse four of Psalm 23 also reminds us that like the Good Shepherd He is, God has a rod and staff to bring us safety, comfort, and guidance. The rod, a heavy, short, straight stick, was a symbol of power and authority. Its purpose was to defend the sheep from predators. The staff was a long, thin piece of wood with a hook at the end. It was used to lean on and to provide rest and peace, but also to guide and correct the flock when they went astray.[1]

As a shepherd himself, David understood the dependance sheep have on the shepherd to provide them with food, water, leadership, and guidance— basically, everything they need to survive. Later in life, David's circumstances gave him reason to *be* the sheep, the one afraid.

Find Your WAY

We can potentially find fear in every part of our known life. But fear can also haunt us in the unknown, as we worry about what "might" happen. It's important to recognize that wherever we go, God goes *with* us. Faith and trust in Him are what take our fears away. If trusting God is how we combat fear, then consider making a list of your fears you can give to God. When you're done, don't go back to dig those fears up. Leave them at the foot of the cross, where the blood that Jesus shed covers them. Here's the reality: bad things do happen to God's people. But the good news is we have God to walk *with* us in our struggles.

You may feel the same fear as you look at the dark world surrounding you. You recognize there are many things you need, but also so much you don't even know you need. The reality is that God knows. And whether you're on the mountaintop or in the valley—a place that might look like uncertainty, discomfort, even death—He's with you. And that changes everything.

Psalm 23 reminds us that God Himself, as the Good Shepherd, is there *with* us to guide us, protect us, and bring us comfort and peace as we journey through the dark valleys of life, whatever those might be.

Reach out to the Shepherd. He's right there with you.

Thank You, Father, for being the Good Shepherd and for knowing me, your little lamb, so well. You not only know who I am, You know exactly what I need. I look to You in complete trust. Guide me on the path I should take, and lead me to where I should go—the good pasture and the restful, quiet waters that I need. Amen.

Wisdom DAY 49

A MEAL OF STRENGTH AND REMEMBRANCE

You prepare a meal for me in front of my enemies. You pour oil of blessing on my head; you fill my cup to overflowing.

PSALM 23:5

A PAINTING THAT HANGS ABOVE the dining room table in our house represents communion to us. The work was created by an artist friend and depicts several jars arranged inside a circle. She explained how she painted the jars as communion cups using an array of colors to represent the diversity of God's Kingdom. The circle around the cups represents the bread. She went on to say that the Lord's table is one of welcome, of worthiness and belonging. She explained that she believes revival happens in one accord, and this piece represents believers coming together despite our differences and our pasts, where we all have a place at His table.

I love having this art in our home above our table because I want our table to host those who are very different from us. Different but still able to find community under the blood of Jesus.

If you are not familiar with Communion, it is the practice of commemorating the death of Christ with bread and wine, which symbolizes His body and His blood. It was while Jesus was eating what was called the Last Supper with His twelve disciples that He took the bread, gave thanks, broke it, and gave it to His disciples, saying, "Take this bread and eat it; this is my body" (Matthew 26:26). Then He took a cup, gave thanks again, and gave it to them, saying, "Every one of you drink this. This is my blood which is the new agreement that God makes with his people. This blood is poured out for many to forgive their sins" (Matthew 26:27–28).

What is amazing to me is that Jesus broke bread that night with those He knew would betray Him. He knew Judas was going to turn his back on Him, and He knew Peter would deny Him. In our lives we might have considered those two people our enemies, but Jesus knew who the real Enemy was and that he would have to be defeated. Jesus was not only able to break bread with Judas and Peter, He even washed their feet that night! Talk about overflow!

As we remember Christ and His sacrifice, our own strength is renewed as we recognize that Jesus gave us Himself to be everything we need—our joy, our strength, our all—despite the pain that He endured. He is our eternal Shepherd. We are to "feed" on Him and His words that give us life and strength.

It's also a treasured reminder that our Enemy, the devil, has already been defeated! The sacrifice that Jesus the Good Shepherd made by dying on the cross for our sins—and the sins of the entire world—is what sealed the devil's fate. The blood He shed as the Lamb of God covered our sins, wiping them out so that we can live in the goodness of His grace, feeling not only unafraid but also fed and blessed beyond measure.

Thank You, Jesus, for paying the ultimate price to give me all I need to live. Even through the hard times, in the middle of what feels like attacks from my "enemies," my hope and trust are in You. Amen.

Find Your WAY

In the past, what have you done when you've felt surrounded by enemies? Maybe it's not one particular person, but a situation or two that caused you to question if God was really there. You may have felt alone or even helpless, like you had no power to change things and were simply being pushed around by your circumstances. In times like these it's important to get back to the basics of who you are in Christ and your position as one of His "sheep." This is the absolute beauty of the Psalms! So many are written to help us call out to God in our distress as they remind us He's fighting for us—and He'll always be victorious!

Wisdom DAY 50

GOODNESS AND MERCY

*Surely your goodness and love will be with me all my life,
and I will live in the house of the LORD forever.*

PSALM 23:6

ON MY TWENTIETH BIRTHDAY I was at church on a Sunday morning, listening to a message about King Solomon. Taken from 1 Kings 3:5–15, the sermon described the story of God appearing to him one night in a dream saying, "Ask for whatever you want me to give you." (Can you even?!) Admitting he was "like a little child," Solomon asked God for wisdom—a "heart that understands" so that he could "know the difference between right and wrong" and wisely rule the people.

The preacher went on to point out the power that came with this young man asking God for wisdom. So from that day on, I made a point to start praying for wisdom! I wanted to live a godly life, and knew I needed God's wisdom to do so. It's why I ask so many people on the podcast about the best piece of advice they've ever been given. I love learning how to live a better life from those who inspire me.

Of course, the best wisdom is found in God's Word. Whether I need courage, strength, hope, truth, or simply to be reminded of how much He loves me, I can find wise words there. As Psalm 63:3 reminds us, God's love is better than life!

This is why we've spent ten weeks focusing on the wisdom books of the Bible—to gain wisdom for living a life that's pleasing to God. Besides being the very best way to live, following God's wisdom is also how the Lord is able to bless you. He has so much good for you! Which brings us to our final verses from Psalm 23.

Goodness and love—or mercy, as seen in other Bible translations—have been likened to two sheepdogs who assist a shepherd with the sheep. As I began to research these animals, I learned that there are actually two types of dogs used on sheep farms: guardian dogs and herding dogs. Guardian dogs help protect the sheep from predators, while herding dogs work with the shepherd to move the sheep where they need to go.[1] It made me think: that's exactly what these two things—goodness and mercy—do for us!

Goodness means obedience to what is right in a way that benefits not just us, but also others. It's doing the right thing for the right reason. Goodness prevents us from doing or saying something harmful, and by its own virtue protects us. Mercy is love and compassion; in essence, it's a gift from God that causes us to take action to help others. Mercy keeps us moving in the right direction.

In the same way goodness and mercy, these two sheepdogs, care for God's flock—whether in the pasture or on the trail. They protect us, draw attention to

Thank You for the goodness and mercy You offer me, and for Your promise to also be with me in heaven where I can live with You forever. Amen.

Find Your WAY

Do you find yourself doubting God's goodness and love? If so, it's often helpful to stop thinking about what isn't going right and start making a list of what is. There's a traditional Cherokee story that describes this concept we've explored: a grandson comes to his grandfather, upset by an injustice done to him. The grandfather tells the boy, "Inside of me there are two wolves. One is good and the other is full of anger. Sometimes it is hard to live with these two wolves inside me, because both of the wolves try to dominate my spirit." The boy asks his grandfather, "Which wolf will win?" The grandfather answers, "The one I feed the most."[2] So, friend, spend time "feeding the wolf" that recognizes what God has done and is doing, and you may find your spirit lifting and your hope rising.

the lost or wounded, and move us where we need to go while keeping the strays from wandering off the path.

What a beautiful picture of how God watches over us. During our time here on the earth, His Holy Spirit abides in us, protecting us and directing us toward the path of life. And as we look through the wide-angle lens of our lives to see eternity, we are comforted by the final promise of this verse—to dwell in the house of the Lord forever. *Forever!* God's Word and His many blessings, both for here and in life ever after, are truly everything you need to find your way.

REFLECT on IT

As you reflect on the week, consider what you've learned about finding your way to the life God has mapped out for you. Highlight the statement(s) below that speak to you, then on the journaling lines write notes to yourself so you can remember God's truth and live it out every day.

- The God of all creation is our personal Guide and Protector who provides everything we need for life.

- In Christ there is rest for the weary, calm for the troubled, and strength for the journey ahead.

- We never need to be afraid, even in the dark times, because the Father is always with us.

- Even when surrounded by trouble, we are strengthened and blessed beyond belief by the Good Shepherd.

- God promises not only that His goodness and mercy will be with us in this life, but that we will live with Him forever in heaven.

_____

_____

_____

REST and WORSHIP

God designed each week to include a day of rest. Use this day to take a time-out from the world and worship Him. Whether it's worship music that helps us turn our eyes and thoughts toward God, or a song that describes exactly how we're feeling, music is a gift that helps connect our spirit with God's Holy Spirit. Here are two of my favorites for this week:

- "Champion," by Maverick City Music, featuring Brandon Lake and Maryanne J. George

- "Gratitude," by Brandon Lake, Bethel Music

Dear God, as I close this week, and this book, I am mindful of the many ways You care for me and the world around me. It's so much more than I can comprehend! From my heart I say: Father of mercy and grace, thank You—for Your Word and Your love, and for showing me wisdom to find my way in this world. But most importantly, the way to live eternally with You. I am overwhelmed with gratefulness! Amen.

One Degree Difference

ALL OF CREATION IS CONSTANTLY IN MOTION, just as God intended and purposed it to move. For instance . . .

- the sun and the moon move the earth in its rotation
- rivers flow to oceans, whose tides ebb and flow
- the wind blows
- grass, flowers, and trees multiply and grow

Everything is moving exactly how it was designed to move. But if any of it gets off course or simply stops, then things begin to go wrong—like, *really* wrong. Much like what happened to the ship *Ever Given* when it became stuck in the Suez Canal.

There's something called the 1-in-60 Rule, which says that for a vehicle traveling sixty miles, a one-degree error will result in that vehicle being one mile off course. If ship captains or plane pilots are off by one degree in their coordinates, it can lead them to tragedy—or, at the very least, pretty far from their original destination.[1]

It's also easy to drift off course in our lives. We fall into the world's patterns and become more like those around us and less like who God created us to be. A choice here, a decision there. A seemingly harmless habit or daily routine. Sometimes these choices are like drifting just one degree. And before we know it, we're headed to the wrong destination.

Maybe you've been there too. Even though you want to live a good, mean-ingful life, you look up one day and realize you're off course. Maybe you're stuck in negative thoughts and habits that make everyday life miserable and ineffective. Maybe you make poor choices that have created unnecessary hardships on yourself and others. Maybe you're simply feeling overwhelmed by life. Whatever it may be, you've lost your way and need help to navigate.

How do we get back on track?

How do we find and move down the path that God intended for us?

The answers lie in the wisdom of God's Word—His truth for living in ways that honor and bring glory to Him, not ourselves.

My prayer for you is that our ten weeks together have sparked a desire to find and follow that truth. It's never a one-and-done process. Proverbs 1:7 says, "The fear of the LORD is the beginning of knowledge, but fools despise wisdom and instruction" (NIV). The key word there is *beginning*. It's now up to you to seek, find, and follow God's desire for you every single day, to become more and more like Christ, and to be His hands and feet to others you meet along the way. God is always ready to meet you with His love, and His Word will always guide you with its wisdom. Consider our final worship song as your reminder . . .

"Goodness of God," by Jenn Johnson, Bethel Music

. . . that God is good and is always, always running after you!

NOTES

INTRODUCTION

1. Yasmine Salam, "Inside the *Ever Given*'s Suez Canal Rescue: How tides, tugboats helped free the big ship," *NBC News*, April 2, 2021, https://www.nbcnews.com.
2. Kit Chellel, Matthew Campbell, and K Oanh Ha, "Six Days in Suez: The Inside Story of the Ship That Broke Global Trade," *Bloomberg*, June 24, 2021, https://www.bloomberg.com.

DAY 2

1. John Chisum, "Chris McClarney: Leading the World in Worship," *Nashville Christian Songwriters*, June 23, 2018, https://www.nashvillechristiansongwriters.com.

DAY 3

1. Tani Kavre, "My Truth," *Urban Dictionary*, April 4, 2017, https://www.urbandictionary.com.

DAY 4

1. Earth Sky Voices, "Why Don't We Feel Earth's Spin?" *EarthSky*, November 17, 2022, https://earthsky.org.

DAY 6

1. "Macchu Picchu," *Encyclopedia Britannica,* February 5, 2024, https://www.britannica.com.

2. Rosie Lesso, "What Are the Seven Wonders of the World?" *The Collector*, December 13, 2021, https://www.thecollector.com.
3. Mark Adams, "Discover 10 Secrets of Macchu Picchu," *National Geographic*, November 6, 2018, https://www.nationalgeographic.com.

DAY 7

1. "New Rules for Macchu Picchu Visit in 2024," *Inca Trail Macchu*, accessed February 12, 2024, https://www.incatrailmachu.com/en/travel-blog/machu -picchu-new-rules-2019.

DAY 9

1. "About C. S. Lewis," C. S. Lewis, the Official Website of C. S. Lewis, accessed February 14, 2024, https://www.cslewis.com/us/about-cs-lewis/.
2. Dane Ortlund, "C. S. Lewis's 1951 Grace Awakening," *The Gospel Coalition*, published August 10, 2010, https://www.thegospelcoalition.org/article /c-s-lewiss-1951-grace-awakening/.
3. James K. A. Smith, *You Are What You Love: The Spiritual Power of Habit* (Ada, MI: Brazos Press, 2016).

DAY 13

1. Sadie Robertson, *Live Original Devotional*, (Brentwood, TN: Howard Books, 2016.)

DAY 15

1. Nicole VanDyke, "Sadie Robertson Huff, Jimmy Darts talk prosperity gospel: It's such a 'shame'" *The Christian Post*, February 13, 2023, https://www.christianpost.com.
2. Ibid.

DAY 18

1. "Tall Poppy Syndrome: When You Get Cut Down for Standing Out," *Newport Institute*, accessed February 12, 2024, https://www.newportinstitute.com.

DAY 19

1. Sadie Robertson Huff, "How to Not Tap Out When Things Get Hard | Sadie Robertson Huff & Nick Vujicic," *WHOA That's Good Podcast*, Apple

Podcasts, January 11, 2023, https://podcasts.apple.com/us/podcast/whoa
-thats-good-podcast/id1433974017.

2. Ibid.

DAY 25

1. Charles R. Swindoll, *David: A Man of Passion and Destiny* (Nashville: Thomas Nelson, 1997), 229.
2. Swindoll, *David,* 231.
3. Swindoll, *David,* 233.

DAY 26

1. Dora Weithers, "Six Habits as Useless as Chasing the Wind," *LetterPile,* updated May 31, 2023, https://letterpile.com.
2. Louie Giglio, "Passion, Purpose, and Designer Jeans," YouTube, December 25, 2014, https://youtu.be/kTCgrP7mJkc.
3. Sadie Robertson Huff, "I Needed My Life to Be Turned Upside Down! | FULL VIDEO with Sadie Robertson Huff & Julie Chen Moonves," *WHOA That's Good Podcast*, YouTube, December 18, 2023, 05:37, https://youtu .be/2rpow77FFho.

DAY 29

1. "What Your Phone Might Be Doing to Your Brain," *UNC Health Talk,* January 5, 2023, https://healthtalk.unchealthcare.org.

DAY 31

1. "Somalia Travel Advisory," *U.S. Department of State—Bureau of Consular Affairs,* accessed February 13, 2024, https://travel.state.gov/content /travel/html.

DAY 37

1. Dr. Daniel Amen, *You, Happier: The 7 Neuroscience Secrets of Feeling Good Based on Your Brain Type* (Carol Stream, IL: Tyndale, 2022).
2. Seth J. Gillihan, PhD, "How Often Do Your Worries Actually Become True?" *Psychology Today*, July 19, 2019, https://www.psychologytoday.com.

DAY 38

1. Erin Blakemore, "Buzz Aldrin Took Holy Communion on the Moon. NASA Kept It Quiet," *History*, July 31, 2018, updated September 16, 2019, https://www.history.com.
2. Bob Roane, "Seeing Ourselves as God Does (Psalm 8)," Words of Hope Bible Ministries, July 5, 2021, https://wohbm.org.
3. "Glory," *Merriam-Webster Collegiate College Dictionary*, accessed February 13, 2024, https://merriam-webster.com.

DAY 39

1. "[GLOBAL ISSUE] Could We Survive Without Insects?" ASEZ, August 8, 2022, https://asez.org.
2. Ethan Brown, "Phytoplankton: How Too Much of a Good Thing Causes Problems," *The Sweaty Penguin*, PBS, October 14, 2022, https://www.pbs.org.

DAY 43

1. "Songs of Songs," BibleProject, February 13, 2016, https://bibleproject.com.
2. Matt Chandler, *The Mingling of Souls: God's Design for Love, Marriage, Sex, and Redemption* (Colorado Springs: David C. Cook, 2015), 17.
3. "Song of Songs."

DAY 44

1. Matthew Henry, *The New Matthew Henry Commentary: The Classic Work with Updated Language,* edited by Martin H. Manser (Grand Rapids: Zondervan, 2010), 944.

DAY 45

1. Dr. Daniel Amen teaches his patients seven principles to keep their relationships healthy and rewarding. They include taking responsibility for keeping your important relationships strong, not taking them for granted, protecting them, clarifying hurts early, noticing what you like more than what you don't, maintaining and protecting trust, and dealing with difficult issues. You can find more detail at https://www.amenclinics.com.

DAY 46

1. Julie Plagens, "Why Jesus compares us to sheep (it's kinda funny)," *Christian Parenting*, October 21, 2020, https://www.christianparenting.org.

2. "Psalm 23, Hebrew Meanings Explained," One for Israel, accessed February 14, 2024, https://www.oneforisrael.org.

3. Max Lucado, *Traveling Light: Releasing the Burdens You Were Never Inteded to Bear* (Nashville: W Publishing Group, 2001), 86.

DAY 47

1. "Slow Me Down, Lord," *Potter's Inn*, October 7, 2019, https://www.pottersinn.com.

DAY 48

1. "Psalm 23:4 Explained: Differentiating the Shepherd's Rod and Staff," *All the Differences*, accessed February 14, 2024, https://allthedifferences.com.

DAY 50

1. "Livestock Protection Dogs," Sheep101.info, accessed February 14, 2024, https://www.sheep101.info/guarddogs.html.

2. "The Two Wolves: A Cherokee Story," Academy of Professional Excellence, San Diego State University, accessed February 14, 2024, https://theacademy.sdsu.edu/wp-content/uploads/2015/06/two-wolves-cherokee-story.pdf.

ONE DEGREE DIFFERENCE

1. Jeff Haden, "The 1 in 60 Rule: How Remarkably Successful People Stay on Track to Accomplish Their Biggest Goals," *Inc.*, May 17, 2022, https://www.inc.com.

ACKNOWLEDGMENTS

Thank you to my family who inspires me every day to make the world a better place for them to live in.

Thank you to the LO team who shows up to work each day with a joyful spirit to reach people with the love of Christ.

Thank you to Debbie Wickwire for writing this book alongside me. Your love for God pours out as you write words and share stories.

Thank you to MacKenzie Howard for helping me with this project from start to finish. Your steadiness and kindness is a blessing to all.

ABOUT THE AUTHOR

Sadie Robertson Huff is a *New York Times* bestselling author, speaker, influencer, and founder of Live Original (LO). Communicating as a sister and friend, Huff is on a mission to use her influence to reach her generation with the message of Christ. Huff is the host of the popular podcast *WHOA, That's Good*, which reached more than a million unique downloads after only fifteen episodes. Her *Live Original* blog features encouraging and transparent messages from Huff and her closest friends. She recently launched her exclusive, online community and app, LO Sister, which is designed to cultivate sisterhood through Bible studies and workshops and also hosts an annual LO Sister Conference. You can learn more about Sadie Robertson Huff at LiveOrginal.com or by following her on Instagram @legitsadierob.